658.4092   SMA   £10.99

Acclaim for *Power Score*

"ghSMART is the world's top firm for helping leaders hire talented teams and run them at full power. Nothing is more important."

—MARSHALL GOLDSMITH, recognized by Thinkers 50
as one of the ten most influential business thinkers in the world,
author of the *New York Times* bestsellers *Mojo* and
What Got You Here Won't Get You There

"I wouldn't be surprised if *Power Score* became the new go-to guide for leadership. Effective teams are key in everything from health care to business to government to nonprofits, and this book will help organizations change the conversation about getting results."

—ATUL GAWANDE, surgeon, author (*Being Mortal,
The Checklist Manifesto*), and executive director
of Ariadne Labs

"*Power Score* offers practical and insightful advice that should be read by anyone leading today's workforce."

—MAYNARD WEBB, chairman of Yahoo!, former chief operating
officer of eBay, and author of *Rebooting Work*

"*Power Score* is an easily understandable process and tool that drives incredible organizational alignment and performance."

—MATT SIMONCINI, president and chief executive officer
of Lear Corporation

"Smart, Street, and Foster have turned more than twenty years of research on leadership into a practical, systematic approach for getting results."

—FREDERICK W. SMITH, chairman and chief executive officer
of FedEx Corporation

"My entire team applied the principles of *Power Score* and has enjoyed explosive growth as a result. Even better, I am having more fun as a leader than ever before."

—JEFF BOOTH, chief executive officer and founder
of BuildDirect

"My team used this approach and got more out of a one-hour conversation than we did in any other strategic planning session we have ever done."

—REGGIE BICHA, executive director of the Colorado Department
of Human Services

"The ghSMART team has done it again. With *Who,* they demystified the process of hiring A Players. Now they have decoded how to become an A+ leader."

—PANOS ANASTASSIADIS, managing partner
of Global Cyber

"I was afraid this would be yet another book telling me the one hundred things I was supposed to do differently. Instead, I was delighted that this book is ridiculously practical."

—JOHN ZILLMER, former executive chairman of Univar

"*Power Score* lays out a practical, straightforward approach to delivering results as a leader. I highly recommend reading it."

—ART COLLINS, former chairman of the board of Medtronic

"Smart, Street, and Foster nailed it—they found the equivalent of the theory of relativity for becoming a top performing leader, a simple, elegant, and practical formula you can put to use immediately in scaling up significant results in your organization. And it's a fun and fast read!"

—VERNE HARNISH, founder of the Entrepreneurs' Organization (EO), chief executive officer of Gazelles, and author of *Scaling Up* and *The Greatest Business Decisions of All Time*

From ghSMART

Power Score: Your Formula for Leadership Success
by Geoff Smart, Randy Street, and Alan Foster

Who: The A Method for Hiring
by Geoff Smart and Randy Street

Leadocracy: Hiring More Great Leaders (Like You)
into Government by Geoff Smart

POWER SCORE

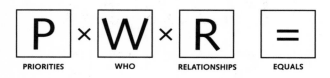

PRIORITIES   WHO   RELATIONSHIPS   EQUALS

POWER

SCORE

*Your Formula for
Leadership Success*

GEOFF SMART, RANDY STREET,
and **ALAN FOSTER**

ghSMART®

P

PROFILE BOOKS

First published in Great Britain in 2015 by
PROFILE BOOKS LTD
3 Holford Yard
Bevin Way
London
WC1X 9HD

www.profilebooks.com

First published in the United States of America in 2015 by
Ballantine Books, an imprint of Random House LLC

1 3 5 7 9 10 8 6 4 2

Printed and bound in Italy by
L.E.G.O. S.p.A. - Lavis (TN)

A CIP catalogue record for this book is available from the British Library.

ISBN 978 1 78125 2147
eISBN 978 178125 2161

Contents

POWER SCORE

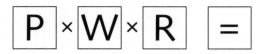

$$\boxed{P} \times \boxed{W} \times \boxed{R} \quad \boxed{=}$$

1

FULL POWER

"The most useful book about leadership." That is what we hope you and your team will say after finishing *Power Score*.

Other books promise this.

That's true, but three things make this one unique.

First, it's based on the largest body of research of its kind. Over the past 20 years, we have conducted in-depth interviews (four hours in length) of more than 15,000 leaders, producing more than 9 million data points.

That's a lot of data!

It is. If you think listening to the advice of *one* leader is helpful, imagine having fifteen *thousand* leaders giving you their best advice!

The Wall Street Journal has called our database "coveted." Research teams from top universities have helped us analyze the data. And the leadership advisors at ghSMART have reflected upon our clients' biggest challenges, and how they have led to success or failure.

We have distilled this research and advice into a simple score that you can calculate with your team. It highlights exactly what you need to do to achieve your goals. We truly believe you will come to see this as the secret formula for success.

What's the second reason this book is useful and different?

We designed this book in "Q&A" format to make it *easy and fun to read*. You talk in bold.

I talk in bold?

That's right, you talk in bold, and we respond. This book is a conversation. We'll tell you what we know and what you need to know, and we'll share some amazing stories—people who turned their companies, their teams, and even their lives around by using the Power Score.

That's a big claim.

It is, but we know that we can back it up.

These ideas have been *battle tested for nearly two decades* in thousands of big companies, entrepreneurial ventures, and even social service agencies. They work. We have even put them into practice ourselves. We'll tell you about times when we have failed and learned so you can avoid our mistakes with your own team.

So what is this book about?

That brings us to the third reason this book is so useful. We provide a simple formula called the Power Score that enables you and your team to identify ways to improve your results.

When your team achieves better results, you will have a more positive impact on the world. You will make a bigger difference for your cause, whatever that might be. And you will enjoy more career success.

My team and I want those things. So what is this "Power Score?"

It's our "grand unified theory of leadership" boiled down to one number, your Power Score.

When you make changes that drive your Power Score up, your results will improve. If you let your Power Score go down, your results will suffer.

How do we calculate our Power Score?

Pull your team together for a Power Conversation—we provide a how-to template at the end of the book to use as a reference. Begin the conversation by asking them, "Are we running at full power?"

Listen to what they say. Their observations will be vague at first, but pay close attention to their comments because they will be your first indication of what you can do differently.

Then ask them to think about three things: P, W, and R.

- P stands for PRIORITIES—Do we have the right *priorities*?
- W stands for WHO—Do we have the right *who*?
- R stands for RELATIONSHIPS—Do we have the right *relationships*?

Ask each team member to rate all three variables on a 1-to-10 scale, with 10 being the top score. Then have them multiply the three numbers together—calculators are allowed!—and hold up their answers.

$$P \times W \times R = \text{Power Score}$$

PWR spells "power." I get it.

Bingo. We made the formula PWR spell "power" to make it easy to remember.

Holding up the scores sounds like a nerve-racking moment! What is a good score?

A perfect score, of course, is 1,000: $10 \times 10 \times 10 = 1{,}000$. But that is nearly impossible. More realistically, a score of 729 or higher means your team is running at full power.

Why only 729?

Because perfection is not a useful goal. You should never feel bad for not achieving perfection, because nobody can do it. We doubt that even Warren Buffett scores a perfect 1,000.

But if your P is a 9, your W is a 9, and your R is a 9, you are doing extremely well.

$$9 \times 9 \times 9 = 729$$

If your team achieves a PWR Score of 729 or higher, we say you are running your team at full power. Congratulations! Great job! Pat yourselves on the back, and keep doing what you are doing. Only about one in ten teams runs at full power at any given time.

If your PWR Score is between 500 and 700, you are still doing pretty well. $8 \times 8 \times 8 = 512$. You are not too far off the mark, and chances are you will find that just a few tweaks will get you to full power. About 30 percent of teams run at this level.

Everybody else falls below 500 and runs well short of full power. If that happens to you, then you have to figure out what or who is dragging your score down and take action to get back to 729 or above.

What do I do with my Power Score once I calculate it?

Once all the people on your team have shared their overall numbers, discuss why they rated each element—P, W, and R—the way they did. This is a critical part of the Power Conversation.

Listen to their ideas to improve the score on each dimension. When you do those things, your Power Score will improve and so will your results.

Who are you three authors? And why should I trust you?

Hi, nice to meet you. We are Geoff, Randy, and Alan. We are business leaders, bestselling authors, and social entrepreneurs.

We are not academics. We are not retired CEOs, and this is not a memoir. We are not self-proclaimed gurus or TV evangelists.

We are three guys who *love* the topic of helping leaders amplify their positive impact on the world. That is why we write books. We are humbled that so many people have read our previous two books, *Who* and *Leadocracy*, making them bestsellers and helping them win awards.

We work at ghSMART, a leadership consultancy.

We have the privilege to serve as the trusted advisors to leaders who own or run large institutions. For two decades, these leaders have called ghSMART to help them hire and develop talented teams that achieve results.

But don't just take our word for it. Here are some other people who have said our approach to leadership has merit:

- Harvard Business School wrote two business school cases titled "ghSMART & Co: Pioneering in Professional Services"
- Atul Gawande praised our disciplined approach to leadership in *The Checklist Manifesto*
- Tom Peters in *The Little Big Things* called our approach to hiring leaders "A BIG damned deal"
- George Anders in *The Rare Find* concluded that, of all approaches to evaluating and selecting leaders, the princples practiced by ghSMART appear to be the most effective
- Maureen Broderick gave us props for being a top firm in *The Art of Managing Professional Services: Insights from Leaders of the World's Top Firms*

Okay, so you seem to know what you are talking about. But does the PWR Score actually work? How much more successful are the leaders who run their teams at full power?

Twice as successful.

Leaders who run their teams at full power are twice as likely to have succeeded in their careers as the average leader. And they are a whopping 20 times more likely to have succeeded than people whose Power Scores are in the bottom 10 percent.

Are you making that up?

Nope. Every number in this book comes from that database and research we mentioned.

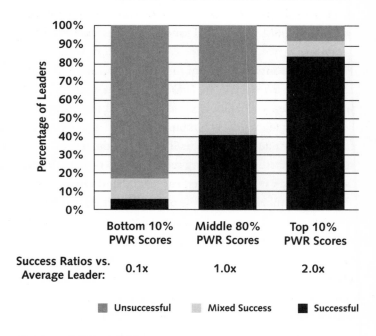

Success Rates Rise with PWR Scores

Note: n = 3,052 candidates
Source: ghSMART proprietary database

Tell me more about your research.

Each of our 15,000 assessments was a semistructured interview that lasted between four and five hours. It covered a leader's entire educational and career history, including jobs held, key accomplishments, failures, strengths, weaknesses, relationships that worked and didn't work, leadership styles, thought patterns, personality traits, and motivations. All told, we collected more than 600 data points per person—more than 9 million data points in all.

Just over a third of those we assessed were CEOs, and the vast majority of the remaining ones were their direct reports or other senior executives. We have also interviewed nonprofit leaders, military generals, school principals, and head surgeons, to give you a sense of the variety of people we have met. PWR is a universal framework for leadership.

After each assessment, we analyzed the data to identify patterns of success and failure. In one assessment, for example, we saw that the candidate had trouble with his father as a child and problems with authority figures throughout the rest of his career. In another, a hard-charging candidate dropped out of school to work in the oil patch and ended up building a massively successful oil services company through a combination of scrappiness, hard work, and exceptional ingenuity. For every assessment we do, patterns emerge that underscore results leaders achieved, behaviors they demonstrated, and motivations that drove them.

All told, we estimate that our team has spent more than 300,000 hours interviewing and analyzing leaders.

Working with Steve Kaplan and his team at the Booth

School of Business at the University of Chicago, we coded more than 3,000 of these assessments to make it easier to study broad longitudinal patterns that apply to leaders across the board.

Working with this data, we began to ask questions such as "What makes a leader successful?" and "What key strengths or weaknesses tend to relate to one another?"

What did you find?

The statisticians crunched the numbers and three distinct groupings of strengths and competencies popped out.

The first included things such as setting vision, devising strategies, and being creative. Not every leader had every one of these strengths, though. That was a surprise at first, but then we discovered something extremely important: It wasn't the *activity* that mattered, but rather the *result*. In this case, whether a leader was deductive or inductive, strategic or more intuitive, each of the successful ones got to the same place: Every one of them set clear *priorities*.

The same goes for the second grouping, which included things such as hiring well, removing underperformers, and developing people. Not everybody did all of these things well, but all the successful ones got to the same result: Each one built a team of A Players mapped against the top priorities. In our language, they were intensely focused on getting the *who* right.

And the final grouping included a wide range of traditional leadership behaviors that forge strong teams—things such as motivating others, following through on commitments, and communicating transparently. The successful leaders didn't set out to practice their leadership skills in a vacuum, though, but rather to foster *relationships* that achieved goals and produced meaningful results.

What's the bottom line?

The key to great leadership is to have the right priorities, the right people on your team, and the right relationships that achieve results: priorities, who, and relationships.

These are the three most important *outcomes* of leadership—what you must accomplish to succeed. Other factors may also contribute to your success, such as luck, interest rates, and the price of tea in China. But of the things leaders control directly, these three matter the most.

PWR is your formula for leadership success. Leaders running their teams at full power, with a top PWR Score, are always more successful than everybody else.

Do I have to do all three to succeed?

You do if you want to run your team at full power. Prioritizing, who, and relationships—PWR—have to work in unison.

Leadership is like a triathlon. Where do you think you will end up if you cannot swim?

At the back of the pack?

Or the bottom of the ocean. You might like running and biking, but you won't win a triathlon if you can't swim.

Good point. So where are leaders weakest?

The most common failure is not having the right people on your team—the W, or who. Fewer than 14 percent of all leaders excel at this. The leaders who do it well are skilled at hiring, removing nonperformers, and developing their teams, and they invest a lot of time in getting it right.

Just under 24 percent of all leaders excel at setting priorities. These leaders tend to be strategic, organized, and decisive. Their priorities connect to their missions, and their teams consider them to be correct and clear.

Percentage of All Leaders Who Excel at P, W, and R

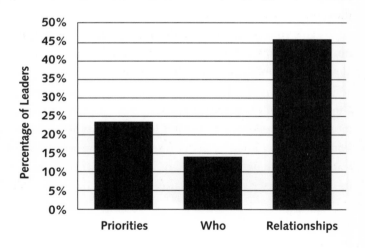

Note: n = 3,052 candidates; leaders who score one standard deviation or greater above the mean on each element
Source: ghSMART proprietary database

What about the R, relationships? I thought leadership was mostly about building relationships and inspiring follower-ship, that sort of thing. That's what most leadership books are all about.

Relationships are important. And yes, that is what most leadership books are about. However, building relationships is the most *common* strength of leaders—47 percent of those in our database excel at it. These leaders ensure that their teams are coordinated, committed to success, and challenged to be their very best.

If you want to be common, just focus on relationships. But if you want to be uncommonly successful, you have to focus on priorities and who is on your team as well.

How many leaders are great at all three—priorities, who, and relationships?

Not many. Only 1 percent of leaders excel in all three—P, W, and R—on a sustained basis throughout their careers. That is a tough standard to achieve week after week and month after month. The good news is that this isn't about being a perfect leader yourself; rather, it's about bringing out the best in your team. Approximately 10 percent of leaders run their teams at full power at any given point in time.

So I want to be in that top 10 percent to operate at full power?

Yes, you do. We'll show you how. But you have to realize that you can't just do the one or two aspects of leadership that you like and skip the rest. You have to do all three.

So let's get started by helping you and your team calculate

your Power Score by accurately rating your P, your W, and your R.

Then let's look at some of the most useful ideas for how you can improve each area.

And finally, let's explore what some of the most successful leaders we have met have done—people with ultrahigh Power Scores—and how you can achieve the same supernova of success when you run your teams at full power.

Ready to dive in?

Ready!

2
PRIORITIES

The triathlon begins?

That's right. Into the water. Flip the goggles down. Time to start swimming.

So P stands for "priorities."

Yes. Simply, priorities are "what needs to be done, and why that matters."

Is that just another word for MBOs or goals? That idea has been around a long time.

True, MBOs—management by objectives—have been around for a long time. Peter Drucker coined the term half a century ago. We were fortunate enough to have had him as a mentor when Geoff started our firm twenty years ago. In fact, Peter helped us craft our business plan.

That's cool.

It was cool. He was a very wise and generous man. Anyway, we are aware that MBOs, or "setting goals," is not a new concept. But we prefer to use the term *priorities* because it's harder and more important than just setting goals blindly.

How so?

Having goals tells you *what* you want to accomplish, but goals alone don't give you any sense of *why* they matter or *which* ones matter most. Setting priorities forces you to focus your energy on the few things that truly count.

We have found that many leaders set goals, but very few have the discipline to set priorities. In fact, 90 percent of the time when a leader is low in "prioritizing," it's because he or she is doing too little of it, not too much of it. People like to keep their options open rather than saying no to unimportant activities.

We worked with one leader who was a brilliant engineer from the Massachusetts Institute of Technology. He helped Amazon build one of the best supply chains in the world, using advanced mathematics to figure out how to get your purchases to your doorstep as economically and quickly as possible. Afterward, he joined a technology start-up and really struggled because he never set clear priorities. As he said, "I was a bit frenetic, thinking about ten things at once. If people needed a lot of direction, they didn't like working with me." Sure enough, his teams found him very frustrating because he didn't know what truly mattered.

Many other teams face similar circumstances. They tell us things like "I see no overriding purpose to what we are doing

day-to-day," or "We are spread too thin," or "We are not focused on the right opportunities," or "We don't make hard decisions around here," or "Senior management may know the
priorities, but nobody else seems to have a clue what they are."

Leaders who neglect to set priorities fail to achieve their
goals. The diffusion of energy drags them down to mediocrity.

Try rating your priorities on a 1-to-10 scale by answering
these three questions:

- Do our priorities *connect* to our mission?
- Do we have the *correct* priorities?
- Are our priorities *clear* to the team?

Priorities that score a 10 are:

- CONNECTED TO MISSION
- CORRECT
- CLEAR

CONNECTED TO MISSION

Tell me more about the first one, connected to mission.

Sure, but this gets a little embarrassing.

Embarrassing?

Our firm ghSMART had recently been written up as a Harvard Business School case study. Two of us, Geoff and Randy,
were seated at the front of an auditorium full of MBA students.

The professor kicked off the discussion by asking a student whether she would work at our firm.

"No, I don't think so," she said and dismissively threw our sixteen-page case to the side of her desk.

"Why not?" the professor asked her.

"As far as I can tell, the firm has no . . . soul."

Really, the student said you had no soul? Ouch!

Yes. It was hard to hear. For Geoff, our founder, this comment felt like a stab to the heart. The blood rushed to his face, and he turned beet red. He was tempted to jump into the conversation and set the record straight—to vehemently tell the student why she was wrong.

Randy was calmer. He smiled and asked the student, "What do you think is missing in this case? What would make you feel that the firm has soul?"

The student explained that she has previously worked at the Peace Corps. "The Peace Corps had taken the time to think about what its members *believed,* what guiding priorities the organization *stood for, why* it existed, what *difference* it made in the world. Has ghSMART taken the time to write these important things down?" Randy looked at Geoff.

"No," Geoff answered, and looked at Randy to see if he agreed.

"No, we haven't," Randy agreed. "But we will. Thank you for your comment."

And you did?

As his first act as managing partner, Randy assembled a town hall meeting to see if the members of ghSMART wanted to tackle capturing what we believed, what we stood for, and why our organization existed. They did. After several all-employee brainstorm sessions, a team composed of new employees and seasoned veterans took a stab at drafting what later became the ghSMART Credo. We had always believed what we wrote, but we had never communicated it before. It took twelve months to finalize our Credo, but it has revolutionized how we think about our work.

It sounds like priorities start with the "why."

Yes. Priorities start with the why and end with the what. Why do you exist and what are you trying to achieve?

Leadership is about helping people derive purpose in their lives, not just getting results out of them. People aren't widgets. They want to know that their efforts contribute to something meaningful and worthwhile. That is why you have to start with the "why."

The afternoon following our visit when we got schooled by the Peace Corps student, we made a second stop in Boston to visit Atul Gawande. He is one of the best leaders we have ever met when it comes to being crystal clear about why his organization exists.

Atul concentrates on public health and is the bestselling author of several books, including *The Checklist Manifesto,* a lifesaving guide to strict operating-room procedures, among other situations. He's still a surgeon in his spare time, and a very busy guy who works in a no-frills office, which was very hot as it turned out, even in the dead of winter.

Anyway, we offered to help him think about the "who" question as he sought to build his research organization.

We asked, "So what do you want to accomplish with your research, and why?"

Atul replied, "We exist to make discoveries that save a million patients from suffering and harm due to health system failure."

The Peace Corps person would have loved his response!

Yes, Atul gets a 10 for clarity of purpose. All of his top priorities tie back to this incredibly motivating "why." For example, one of his biggest ones is to build a world-class research team capable of identifying ways to save patients on a broad scale.

But isn't all this a lot easier in the not-for-profit sector? Fortune 500 CEOs are bottom-line driven.

You're putting the "what" *before* the "why"! It doesn't matter if you're trying to save the world or save a company (and its jobs)—people need a motivating "why" to do their best work. The "what" will follow.

We have seen many for-profit leaders connect to their mission just as passionately as Atul Gawande does. Josh Silverman, the former CEO of Skype, for example.

After eBay purchased Skype for $2.6 billion, the media and analysts screamed that the price tag was way too high. The company had gone through four CEOs in four years. Josh would be the fifth, and the pressure on him to perform was immense.

"That made for a stressful start!" he told us. "Morale was low when I came in. The focus from investors, the press, and leadership had been on hitting artificially inflated financial projections. This sent a message to the team that they were failing."

Josh knew he had to engage his team even before he had gotten to the root of the problem. He started by inviting customers to the company to share what Skype meant to them; most shared how free phone calls over the Internet had given them a close, personal connection with someone far away.

Phone calls? I thought Skype was in the video conference business. People use it as a verb—like "I will Skype you tonight."

That is how we think about it today, but that was not always the case. Video was a minor feature buried in the product when Josh first arrived.

"We realized that video should be the centerpiece," Josh said. "People have been talking about making video calls since *The Jetsons,* and we were uniquely positioned to do something about it. Nobody was doing it, and everything was coming together, like broadband, to make it work. I gave our team until the end of the year to ship this product with video as the front-running feature."

Skype repositioned the brand around video when the product came out. It helped that news programs starting using it to speak with people around the world, and Oprah Winfrey began to have live conversations with viewers of her show. Although the audio product never went away, people came to know Skype as a video conferencing service.

Elevating video gave Josh an opportunity to rethink the

mission, too. "We shifted our positioning from 'free phone calls' to 'bringing people together when they couldn't be together in the same room.' All I had to do is expose people to the mission by introducing them to customers on video so they could tell their stories."

You're losing me.

We'll let Josh explain how he connected his priorities to the mission for his team.

"I brought in people from the UN who were staffed abroad in refugee camps for eighteen months without seeing their family. I had soldiers call in from the other side of the world. I'd have them on video during our town hall meetings to tell us how much Skype meant to them and their families. The electricity—the energy—that this connection to mission created really propelled us to grow the company, because everyone was crystal clear on why we were there."

Focusing on video as the top priority and connecting people to the mission turned out to be wildly successful. Under Josh's tenure, Skype became the global leader for videoconferencing. The value of the company grew from $2.6 billion to $8.5 billion in just three years. That's close to a 50 percent annual growth rate.

Awesome.

Yes, here is another awesome story of connecting to mission. Art Collins was CEO of the medical device company Medtronic. He was watching a surgeon get prepped for surgery and, suddenly, out came the brain drill.

Did you say brain drill?

Yes, it's what you think it is. We never said leading is easy! So Art watched as a surgeon drilled a small hole into the skull of his patient and inserted a Medtronic neurostimulation device.

The patient was a concert pianist who suffered from Parkinson's disease. His hands shook so badly, he could no longer play the piano.

"I sat there watching this patient whose hands had been shaking uncontrollably suddenly stop shaking," Art told us. "It worked. When the neurostimulation device was in the right place, he just stopped shaking. It was instantaneous. It was like a miracle had just happened."

The concert pianist later came to a Medtronic holiday party in Europe. The man explained that he was still afflicted by Parkinson's, but thanks to Medtronic, he was able to do something he had not been able to do for years. He sat regally in front of the grand piano on the stage and played for all of the employees.

"That was a really unique and special moment," Art recalled. "That did more to connect our team to our mission than anything I could have ever said or done."

Art added, "In another case, a girl in her mid-teens with severe scoliosis shared how our device—actually a series of devices—had enabled her spine to come into perfect alignment without having to suffer an ugly long incision down her back. Our product worked with some very small incisions, almost like a keyhole. She beamed when she told our employees that she was able to wear a backless gown to her high school prom."

Okay, I get it. It's important to think about why you exist and to remind your team about the positive impact your work is making on the world.

Yes—more than important; it's critical. But that's not the only thing you have to worry about with priorities.

You have to make sure your priorities are correct.

CORRECT

What do you mean priorities have to be correct?

They have to be the right ones—the short list of things that you believe will enable you to achieve your big goals. If you think the odds are high that you will get what you want by accomplishing your priorities, then they are probably correct.

Unfortunately, it's rarely obvious what the right priorities are when you are in the thick of it. Yet these are the things you are betting on—the outcomes that matter most.

What are some examples?

The "what" of priorities typically have to do with choices regarding customers, employees, products, places, competitors, suppliers, and anything else of strategic importance. Setting special goals or outcomes must accompany the priority to make it real.

Here are a few examples to give you an idea of what we mean.

- *European expansion:* Grow our customer base in
  Europe from 3 to 10 customers, and from $3 million
  to $10 million in revenue, within 18 months.
- *Customer mix:* Reduce our reliance on residential
  customers by growing commercial customers from
  20 percent of our revenue to 60 percent within
  2 years.
- *Product:* Concentrate 75 percent of our R&D resources
  on "Project Bluebird" and win at least two major industry quality awards within 3 years.

**These make sense. They describe a specific outcome and in-
clude some goals and timelines to help describe it.**

Exactly.

What does this have to do with being correct?

Outcomes such as these will focus you on what you must
accomplish to succeed. You should be able to see the link between the outcomes and your ultimate goals.

Not only that, but the specificity of your outcomes will help
you stay on top of your priorities as things change. Your priorities might need to evolve to stay on the right trajectory.
That is what Larissa Herda faced as she moved her organization through two economic recessions.

Larissa was the CEO of tw telecom, a joint venture between
Time Warner and US West. As a first-time CEO, she focused
on building a strong team that would offset her lack of experience. "I knew what I didn't know, which at that point was a lot,
so what I did was put people in key leadership positions that I

thought would compliment my strengths and shore up my weaknesses." This proved critical to her success.

The company was still small when the 2001–2002 recession hit, so when big telecommunications carriers that were customers went bankrupt, tw telecom had to lay off a third of its workforce. "It was one of the most devastating experiences of my professional life," she said.

It also proved to be a valuable lesson. Larissa and her leadership team monitored the market very closely over the next few years and steadily grew the business. "We listen and talk to a lot of people. We talk to employees and customers. I personally read prolifically—several newspapers a day. Business was growing nicely, we were successfully integrating a large acquisition, we were approaching double-digit revenue growth, and we were hiring aggressively, but in the fall of 2007 we could see that something was going on in the capital markets. There was stuff going on with corporate paper that was bad. Things were starting to occur that weren't quite major headlines yet."

Keeping the previous recession in mind, the team debated the facts and ultimately came to the difficult but deliberate decision to change their focus. Their plan had been to invest in people for growth. Now, they decided to stop all hiring.

That is a dramatic shift in priorities. How did the company respond?

Understandably, most people at tw telecom were shocked. Things were going so well and they felt they could not handle the growing workload without more people. But Larissa and her leadership team could see storm clouds on the horizon.

Their bold action paid off. The Great Recession hit. While

other companies started bleeding, tw telecom actually grew its top and bottom line during that period, and as Larissa proudly said, "We did it without layoffs!" From 1997 to 2012, the company grew from $26 million in revenue to $1.4 billion. That is more than 30 percent per year for fifteen years. When tw telecom went public, many employees shared in the upside.

We credit Larissa and her team with realizing that tw telecom's priorities were incorrect in 2007. By resetting those priorities before the recession, she helped her entire team win.

Reading the markets right is pretty iffy. How else can people make sure they have the correct priorities?

The best way is to pay very close attention to your customers and competitors. That is what Aaron Kennedy had to do.

It had been raining for thirty straight days in Madison, Wisconsin, but it may as well have been raining for a year. Twenty-eight-year-old Aaron Kennedy had maxed out his credit cards with $50,000 in debt to open two Noodles & Company restaurants one thousand miles apart. One was in Denver and the other in Madison. Both were losing money at an alarming rate.

"Both restaurants had gotten off to a really fast start and then customer traffic began to trail off quickly," Aaron said. "So my team and I drove through the rain to Chicago to study the burgeoning Asian noodle shops there and returned to the Madison store to do some taste testing.

"Our Madison restaurant was in this beautiful, turn-of-the-century, redbrick building on State Street," Aaron said. "We assembled in the upstairs dining room and had the staff bring us one noodle dish at a time for us to taste and critique.

"After the first couple of dishes, a few from the group com-

mented that each dish was worse that the previous one. Noodles & Company definitely was not delivering on the vision for
the brand!

"About halfway through this tasting, a staff member
sprinted up the back staircase and burst into the upstairs dining room. We were the only ones sitting there, and the staff
member told us that water was pouring into the basement."

Seven increasingly bad dishes in a row had left the group
wary of trying more, so they were very happy for the diversion.
They raced downstairs to the dank basement to find water
flooding through a hole in the old wall. They grabbed a bunch
of Slim Jim garbage cans and used them to scoop the water off
the floor. A few people hauled each filled garbage can upstairs
and dumped it downstream from the hole in the building
while the rest continued to scoop and fill another garbage can.

"Here we were, scooping and pouring, scooping and pouring," Aaron remembered.

Did the flood bring the team together, or drive them apart?

It almost drove them apart for good! But Aaron rescued the
situation.

When the rain subsided, the sweaty and exhausted group of
seven made their way out of the basement. Six of them were
ready to escape before their reputations were tainted. They
had driven to Chicago, toured restaurants, driven home, eaten
bad noodles, commiserated over a poorly executed vision, and
scooped a small swimming pool out of the basement of a
hundred-year-old building. They were done. They were as
soggy as the noodles they ate and ready to quietly extract
themselves from the Noodles & Company adventure forever.

"I felt like this was the most critical juncture in Noodles & Company's history," Aaron said. "It was about to die on the operating table. Everybody wanted to leave, but this was my moment to either bail out with them or to step in and galvanize the team and resuscitate the patient. I said, 'Let's go back upstairs. Let's define what needs to be done and let's fix this company.'"

Resetting priorities actually prevented people from quitting?
More than that—it saved the company. "It was like we knew the current plan was not going to get us there," Aaron told us, "so we threw it out."

The group trudged back to the dining room and began to recount everything they had learned that day. Aaron continued, "Everyone debated what mattered most, and we settled on a very specific set of new priorities that gave us all new energy."

Before long, they had drawn up a list of fifteen ideas that revolved around three priorities:

1. making the environment more comfortable and inviting,
2. changing the basic customer flow/ordering process, and
3. improving the food.

They laid out a timeline and agreed to tackle the list together.

Today, Aaron Kennedy is very proud of his team and the company they built. The company has over 400 locations in 28 states, and grossed over $400 million in 2013.

As Aaron reflected on the experience, he realized that his team's "day in the rain" was the inflection point for the company. "I think success requires more than just hard work," he said. "It requires the combination of a clear vision and the perseverance to pursue it. I don't think all leaders understand what they are trying to build, and so they don't convey it in an impactful way. Without that, people don't know what to do. We figured out the priorities that mattered, and it saved the business."

So, if my priorities are correct, am I all set?

No, there is one more thing. Your priorities must be clear.

CLEAR

What makes them unclear?

The most common reason is having too many priorities. That is why most leaders struggle with a low P score. They never say no and allow too many priorities to creep in.

Prioritizing means making decisions, and a lot of leaders are afraid to do that. It makes them vulnerable. Saying yes to one thing means saying no to another, and that will surely upset somebody on the team. It's easier to just go with the flow or to pay consultants to make hundred-page strategy presentations. In the end, a lot of leaders want to avoid having to make an actual choice about what matters and what doesn't because choices have consequences.

Only 9 percent of all leaders truly excel at making decisions, particularly those that eliminate options.

Recently, we worked with the leadership team of one of the largest direct service charities in the United States. They had a clear vision, a passionate team, and a thriving culture.

They also had 164 annual organizational priorities. Not surprisingly, they were exhausted. Who can deliver on 164 priorities? After much discussion, they pruned the list the next year to 76 priorities, which is still way too long. The COO ran the cumbersome process and said, "We are an inclusive organization. We want everyone to feel that their goals are also a priority for the organization." By trying to be nice, they had ended up with confusion and too much going on.

Too many priorities means you have zero priorities.

That sounds painful. Who does it well?

Maynard Webb is great at prioritizing.

His story is fascinating, too. He eventually became one of the most celebrated leaders in the high tech world, and he wrote the popular book *Rebooting Work*.

But his career started quite humbly. Some people start in the mailroom. Maynard started out as a security guard.

As in cybersecurity?

No, as in "sitting behind the reception desk, giving you a name badge" security. He started as a security guard at IBM and grew into a very successful career in IT. Eventually, he became president of eBay Technology and later chief operating officer for Meg Whitman when eBay was having some severe growing pains.

Was that when eBay's servers kept going down?

Yes! And Maynard was the leader Meg brought in who got them back up and running, which was no small feat.

He did it mostly by prioritizing.

He's like a firefighter who runs straight into fires and figures out quickly what to do to put out the whole fire rather than focusing on the first brushfire he comes across.

Maynard said, "I have always taken jobs that everybody else was running away from because I was always confident I could do it." His CEO was so confident that he could solve the problem that she wanted to include a slide at an analyst presentation that said simply: "Maynard Webb hired. Problem solved."

What was his secret to success?

Maynard saw that his team members were focusing more on putting out the fires in front of them than they were on getting out in front of the real problem. On his third official day of work, he asked them a seemingly simple question: "When do we hit the wall?"

They didn't understand what he meant. He asked it another way: "When do we run out of capacity? I know we can't keep the site up right now and we want to add redundancy to fix that, but we are a fast-growing company. Even if we get the site up and running, when do we actually run out of capacity?"

His team had no idea. Nobody had ever thought to ask that question before. They were so mired in the weeds that they had never stopped to look up and evaluate it for themselves. When would eBay's growth outstrip what their servers could do, even if the site was up at the moment?

After three more days, they came back to Maynard with an

answer: The site had three weeks to live. Maynard's response: "That was not the answer I was hoping for!"

Whoa! What did he do?

Maynard said, "I made it simple for people and boiled it down to four priorities. First, we are going to fix our capacity issues. It is not good to have our site down, and I am not a fan of CNN in my parking lot, so we are going to fix that. That one was pretty clear. Second, we need to scale. It is not enough to keep the lights on. We need to grow with the company. Third, we are going to innovate at the same time. This was not a traditional approach, but we had to get out in front. We called it velocity, and it meant asking for twice the money while delivering four times as many features. Fourth, we are going to save money so we can invest in more product development."

It sounds as if he limited his focus to only four priorities.

That's right. He focused on the four things that truly mattered to eBay at that point in time. He made it perfectly clear for his team.

What Maynard did seems relatively straightforward in hindsight, and yet nobody had done it before him. His team was so busy putting out the brushfires that they had lost the forest for the trees. By asking the right question—when do we hit the wall?—and deriving the right priorities from it, Maynard was able to put eBay's technology on the right track. The rest, of course, is history.

What should I do if my team has a hard time focusing?

You could try what Claire Bennett did.

When Claire first became head of the travel business for American Express, profits were sagging and employee morale was taking a similar turn. When she looked across the business operations, it became clear that the different areas—such as frontline travel advisors, online booking management, marketing, and product development—were going in many different directions. This unintentionally caused silos and misalignment with priorities. Customers who were used to the high-touch service of American Express weren't fully satisfied because they felt they were being pressured into buying something other than what they wanted, and that bothered them.

Claire gathered her team together to list every priority they could think of on a whiteboard. The list had more than twenty items on it, including some product offerings that only 5 percent of customers used. "Why are we focusing on areas that will never be of interest to a majority of our customers?" Claire asked. Beyond margins, nobody could offer a good answer. She cut those items from the list.

She continued to ask questions that pitted one item against the next, ultimately winnowing the list down to five priorities. They all revolved around the customer's experience. One priority was to drive simple transactions, like airplane reservations, to the Web so travel advisors could focus on more complex trips that required a personal touch and greater expertise. Another was to place renewed focus on helping customers with lodging reservations on those more complicated trips. "What is more fun for a travel advisor," Claire asked, "booking a plane ticket or booking somebody's dream trip to Africa?"

Claire told her team that those five priorities were the only ones they would discuss in weekly meetings. Even still, her leaders often came to her with ideas outside these core five. Claire held the line. "If you are doing something that is not a priority, then make a good case as to why we need to pivot. If it is not about these five things or you can't show me why it is in the best interest of our customers, then we should not be doing it."

Did it work?

It did. The consumer travel division's Recommend a Friend statistic jumped from around 40 percent to 70 percent, and team satisfaction reached one of the highest levels in the entire company. Profits grew tenfold. Most important, Claire had restored American Express Travel to the shining star of customer service that epitomizes the brand.

SETTING PRIORITIES

When should a team set priorities?

You can set them right when you start a job, as Maynard and Claire did, or you might use a crisis to reset your priorities, as Aaron did. Or, like Larissa, you may realize the market is shifting and make a change then.

How do teams set priorities?

Lots of ways.

Take Kristin Russell. She's an information technology celebrity executive who was recruited to run IT for the state of

Colorado. She set priorities by talking to users of the systems she was charged with managing.

"Technology is actually pretty easy," Kristin said, "but people are hard. It is like the Lewis Carroll quote, 'If you don't know where you are going, any road will get you there.' I needed to figure out what road we were on, and the only way to do that was talk to the people who actually used our system. Once I knew that, I knew where to focus my team. We took six months and identified the five priorities that mattered most— including reducing the number of IT systems so that all divisions of the government could communicate, collaborate, and automate."

Indeed, Geoff just updated his driver's license, and a process that once required two hours to drive to a DMV office and wait in line now took only two minutes and twenty-four seconds.

Talking to customers and working with my team seem like a good options. How do I do that practically?

Try getting into the field more. That is what Jim Donald did before he took the job as CEO of Extended Stay Hotels. He wanted to have a point of view about what mattered most. Guess how many hotels he visited before taking the job. Forty. That gave him the perspective he needed to form his priorities.

Bill George did the same thing. He is a professor of management practice at Harvard Business School, where he has taught leadership since 2004. But he's also the author of four bestselling books and the former chairman and chief executive officer of Medtronic before Art Collins. "You have to be an engaged leader with customers and pay attention to detail. Be out there in the marketplace. Be at the point of distribution. Be at the trade shows at eight A.M. with the doctors. This is not micromanaging. It is knowing your customer. I saw seven hundred procedures in Europe, the U.S., and Africa."

What do I look for in the field?

Focus your attention on your customer's needs. That should lead you to your biggest priorities.

A few years ago, Motorola asked Juergen Stark to run the Razr phone rollout in Japan. After being on the ground and talking to his local team for a day, he realized that the phone lacked the technical capabilities to meet any of the ten highest-priority needs of the local customers.

Juergen said to his new team, "Why are you surprised that people who buy our phones return them 50 percent of the time? These aren't minor technical details, but major things our consumers want. No matter how much marketing we do, the phone will never sell." Even worse, adding those features would have been cost prohibitive.

Juergen changed the priority from "how to market the phone in Japan" to "how to wind it down as quickly as possible." He said, "At the end of the day, you have to focus on the consumer and what the consumer is going to buy or not buy. Nothing else really matters. Everyone can agree on your strategy and be supportive—your supply chain, your distributor, your buyer, your sales team—but if you don't have a product the consumer will actually buy and you don't understand the details of what that consumer wants, then the rest of it makes no difference."

What if my priorities end up being wrong?

It's common to have the wrong priorities, and if they are, you will know soon enough.

We know of one business leader who made a courageous change to his priorities in the prime of his career.

After several decades of building a large and successful business, this entrepreneur gave up his operating role while continuing to serve as chairman of the board. Unfortunately, he became bored. And stressed. The day-to-day hassles of being tied to this business were like an anchor that prevented him from moving on to the next chapter of his impressive career. In addition, his marriage had dissolved. He felt stuck in his career and in his life. If he had not reexamined his priorities, this entrepreneur might have just remained on the board, feeling bored, stressed, and stuck. He would not have had the mental bandwidth to advance to the next stage of his career and personal life.

Instead, he had an epiphany. He told us, "The point is this: You're not going to find what you're looking for until you leave the port you're stuck in." He took bold action. To the surprise of many, he decided to resign from the board of the company he had founded. This one decision freed up his mind and calendar for what came next. He was able to increase his philanthropic efforts, complete some very creative projects that brought joy to millions, and, yes, move on and eventually find the love of his life.

At his wedding reception, with fireworks casting a warm glow on the man, his new wife, and family and friends, this entrepreneur, whose face used to show signs of strain and preoccupation, looked very "present" and peaceful. Years later, he reports that he still feels present and peaceful. It is amazing how life-changing it can be to courageously and consciously change a priority.

That's great. Okay, I get it on priorities. They start with the why and end with the what. They need to be connected to the mission, correct, and clear. Now, how can my team *rate* our priorities?

The easiest way is to sit down with your team and list your priorities on a whiteboard. Rate them on a scale of 1 to 10.

Are they connected to the mission? In other words, will pursuing these particular priorities help us fulfill our mission?

Are they correct? Can we link them to our broader goals?

Are they clear? Does everybody understand them? Do we have the right number to keep us focused?

After rating each one, look at the whole list and ask, "Do we have the right priorities?" Give yourselves an overall score from 1 to 10.

RATE YOUR TEAM'S PRIORITIES
"I think our P = _____ on a scale of 1 (low) to 10 (high)."

SCALE	DESCRIPTION	CHECK THE BOX THAT DESCRIBES YOUR PRIORITIES
1	"We have not thought about our priorities at all." "We are just doing stuff, without a sense of what is expected or why."	☐
2	"We have thought just a little bit about our priorities, but we are not sure they are the right ones." "There is no consensus about what our priorities should be."	☐
3	"We have a vague sense of what we want to achieve, but it's not specific."	☐
4	"We have spent some time clarifying our priorities, but we are not in agreement that we have the right ones or that other people in our organization know what they are."	☐
5	"We have a general sense of what we are trying to accomplish, but we have not discussed or debated enough to know if they are the right priorities."	☐
6	"We have priorities, but there are too many of them" or "too few of them" or "We are not focused on the right things."	☐
7	"Some people might know what the priorities are, but not everybody."	☐
8	"We have healthy discussion and debate about what our priorities are, and we are almost in full agreement that we are on the right track, but we have not yet connected the priorities to everyone's job."	☐

| 9 | "We have clarified our priorities, they are the right ones, and we are in the process of linking them to everyone's roles and goals." | ☐ |
| 10 | "Our priorities have been widely discussed, debated, agreed upon, and communicated. They connect to our mission, are the correct ones to achieve our broader goals, and we are all crystal clear about them." | ☐ |

3
WHO

So this is the bike part of the triathlon?

Yup. Dry off and mount up!

What is the essence of who?

It means hiring the right people onto your team and matching them to the right priorities.

How important is that?

It is the single most important thing you can do. Who you have on your team, and who is in your organization, will determine your success more than anything else.

The Wall Street Journal, in its review of *Who,* wrote that this issue of the who—hiring the right people—is the "most important aspect of business." And the numbers bear that out.

The number-one, most common weakness leaders have is in failing to remove underperformers. The fourth most common weakness leaders have is in hiring A Players.

Interestingly, leaders who are good at removing under-performers are also good at hiring A Players. It's as if a leader either "gets it" that talent matters or doesn't think that way at all.

Yeah, it's about getting the right people on the bus and into the right seats. That's what Jim Collins says.

And he's right. As one person at a recent PWR talk pointed out, "You can't have a high P or a high R if you don't have a high W. You have to have the right people to hope to have the right priorities and the right relationships."

In our client organizations, by far the one thing that gives leaders the most heartburn is the W, the who. One of our clients joked, "Leadership is pretty easy. Except for the people part."

Okay, so say I want to get good at who. What do I need to do?

To score a 10 on the W, try asking these three questions:

- Have we *diagnosed* our team to understand its strengths and risks?
- Have we *deployed* the right people against the right priorities?
- Have we *developed* our team?

A strong W score results when you have:

- DIAGNOSED
- DEPLOYED
- DEVELOPED

DIAGNOSED

That seems straightforward enough. How does it work?

Two words: *Who matters.*

Too many leaders facing a problem start with the *what.* They begin by micromanaging and making decisions about *things*—processes, products, pricing, customers, and so on. For example, we met one plant manager who told us about a bunch of equipment failures he had in the factory. "I had to spend a lot of time working through those. As it turns out, we could have prevented most of the problems if we had the right people in the first place. I didn't see that fast enough."

The better approach is to focus first on getting the right people on your team to achieve your priorities. Ask yourself, "Do I have the right who?"

Verne Harnish is a great example of someone who has always recognized the power of that question. He co-founded a group called the Association of Collegiate Entrepreneurs when he was a young MBA student at Wichita State University in 1983. He had this idea to create a list of the top 100 entrepreneurs under the age of thirty, but he had no idea how to do it, and this was long before the Internet would make something like this easy. Then he realized that "how" was the wrong question. He asked his team, "Who has already been down this road we are about to travel?" That led them to John Naisbitt, author of *Megatrends,* who helped them build their list.

When Verne wanted to get media attention for the group, he again asked, "Who is the smartest person in the world when it comes to marketing?" That led him to Regis McKenna, who helped Apple, Intel, and Genentech with their marketing in the early days.

Verne later launched the Young Entrepreneurs Organization (now known as Entrepreneurs' Organization, or EO) and Gazelles, a company that helps midmarket companies execute their strategic plans. His take: "I think what you have really got to do as a leader is set your ego aside and admit that you don't have the answers. You just have to ask the right question, and it is always a who question, not a what or a where or a how one. Once you know the answer to that, go ask that person for help."

What about the team I already have? Wouldn't that be the most logical place to start looking for the right who?

That's a great place to start. Ask yourself how confident you are that you have a team of A Players who can accomplish your priorities.

You want to be 90 percent or more confident.

That seems unrealistic.

Not at all. We work with leaders all the time who improve their confidence—and the likelihood of their team to perform—from 50 percent to 90 percent. They build teams full of A Players.

But wouldn't all those A Players compete with one another?

They would if you hired a bunch of prima donnas. We don't define A Players that way, though. We define A Players as those who have at least a 90 percent chance of succeeding in a role where only the top 10 percent of possible people could succeed, at a given compensation level.

If you need people to work together as a team, then make that part of the job—part of the definition for what an A Player looks like to you. So if you have somebody that competes with the rest of the team, then that person isn't an A Player at all. See how that works?

Aha! A Players are relative to my expectations for the job.

That's right. They are an A Player only if they can accomplish the priorities of the job—and do it in your company, on your team, and with you as the leader. An A Player in one job or on one team might be a C Player in a different job or on another team.

So how to do I figure that out?

List your priorities, match them to the people who will play a role in completing them, and rate your team's likelihood of achieving them. Anything short of 90 percent means you have work to do.

Panos Anastassiadis does this very well. He was the CEO of Cyveillance, which grew more than 1,500 percent in five years.

Panos shared how he thought about the who in his business when he told us the following: "Every quarter I start with a blank sheet of paper and design an organizational chart based on my biggest priorities. I make the assumption that I have to operate with only 50 percent of my staff. Who would be on my team? Then I increase my assumption to 70 percent, 85 percent, and 95 percent. Immediately, I know who my stellar personnel are and who are key and indispensable. Whoever is not in the 85 percent group is very dispensable, and I average-up on the first occasion. As a result, our voluntary attrition has been less than 2 percent."

That sounds aggressive.

It is. Panos was one of the Cheetahs we studied for *Who*— a group of CEOs who are persistent, efficient, and proactive. They have incredibly high standards and always move quickly on who issues. They are among the most successful CEOs in the world.

We gave Panos a stuffed cheetah as a thank-you for being in our last book. He keeps it in his office to this day. "This who stuff works!" he quipped. "The cheetah is a constant, daily reminder of the importance of having the right team. The team we built has been the single decisive factor for our success. I have been simply following your teachings of constantly averaging-up who is on the team."

Are there other ways to diagnose my team?

You probably already know intuitively where the issues are on your team, but you can use the skill-will bull's-eye if it helps.

Huh?

It is a simple framework with two questions. First ask yourself if each person on your team has the *skill* to do the job. We are not talking about doing the activities of the job, but actually getting the results you want. Can they accomplish the priorities?

Second, ask if each person has the *will* to do the job. Do

they believe in your mission and are they motivated to be on your team?

A Players are the people who have both the skill and the will. They are in the skill-will bull's-eye.

What if someone has the skill but not the will? Shouldn't I keep him and hope he or she will find some other way to get motivated?

No, although we can see why you would be tempted down that path. We have worked with several clients who were reluctant to remove their top-performing salesperson because they didn't think they could absorb the loss. The problem was that the person was toxic to their culture.

In the end, they finally asked those people to leave. Amazingly, in every case, the remaining team was so relieved that they rallied to fill the sales gap. None of these companies missed a beat.

Couldn't I just reassign the person?

Maybe, if the person wants to do the new job. Think about whether the will gap is due to a disconnect with your mission or with the daily task of the job itself. If it is just the job, you might be able to solve your problem with a reassignment. If the gap is with you, your team, or your priorities, you will need to take action to move that person out.

Remember Claire Bennett of American Express Travel? Well, she inherited seven people, some of whom were unsupportive of the new priorities. She tried to encourage them to get on the bus for a while, but finally asked them to go if they could not support the new priorities. As she told us, "The remaining team members came to me and said, 'Why did it take you so long?' That was a great lesson. I wish I had moved faster on some of them. I wanted to give them every chance to get on board, but once it was clear they were never going to get there, I should have moved them out sooner."

What about someone who has the will, but lacks the skill? It seems like a positive that the person wants to be on my team.

Well, that individual would still be a B Player at best because he can't do the job you need him to do. But if you can find a role that matches his skills better, you might be able to turn him back into an A Player.

Mike D'Ambrose discovered this when he first went to Archer Daniels Midland Company as its new chief human resources officer. Early on, he ran a talent review process using a classic 3x3 grid that maps people's performance versus potential. High performers with high potential end up in the top right box, and low performers with low potential end up in the bottom left box. But, running the process at his new company caused Mike to rethink everything he knew about talent.

"I put this giant nine-box on the wall, ten feet long and nearly as high, and velcroed people's names into different boxes. I brought in our leadership team, and we spent hours moving people around and discussing them. What they told me about the lower boxes got me thinking about everything I knew about HR. I expected them to want to fire everybody in those lower boxes. Instead, they asked, 'How did we get those good people in the wrong jobs?' We spent the rest of the meeting thinking about where they could perform as A Players in our company."

That gives me some good ideas. I need to diagnose my team by thinking about both skill and will relative to my priorities—the "what" and the "why." If I go through this exercise and realize I have some B and C Players, what do I do then?

Now you need to move to the second step: ensuring each person is properly deployed.

DEPLOYED

Sounds like a military operation. What's involved?

Three things. First, you have to remove your underperformers. Second, you need to move people around to get them in the right jobs. Lastly, you need to hire A Players to round out your team.

Let's start with removing underperformers. If you know you have the wrong people in place, you have to take action. Remember those top 1 percent PWR leaders we mentioned? They are six times more likely to remove people than everybody else, and that has been key to their success.

Bill Amelio found himself in this situation when Lenovo put him in charge as CEO. You may remember that Lenovo is the Chinese company that purchased IBM's personal computer business and ThinkPad brand in 2005. Anyway, Bill inherited a company that was losing money hand over fist, and he decided to change the majority of his team.

Bill needed to eliminate all of the shadow products—people's pet projects—that were driving up costs. "I decided to go with a geographic approach to the P&L to drive accountability and ultimately better control profits. We focused everything on regional P&Ls. Then I realized that many of the leaders could not make this transition and had to go. In the end, we changed out 70 percent of our leadership team. IBM was great at creating products and had solid management development except when it came to poor-performing leaders; the company took far too long to make a change when a leader was failing. The culture we created at Lenovo was more aggressive on change and highly performance based. I needed people who understood that."

Bill began to act on his team, removing people who lacked either the skill or will to perform in this new environment.

It worked. The new leadership team he put in place took Lenovo from the fifth-largest PC maker to number one in the world at the time.

What about moving people around? That's classic deployment.

Exactly. As we said earlier, sometimes you have the right people on your team, but they are in the wrong jobs. They are miscast, like actors playing the wrong roles or athletes in the wrong positions. You know they have talent, but you need to move them to different roles to set them up for success. Or they might have been in the right role at one time, but changing circumstances require a different skill set.

Jim Goodnight is quite good at that. He is the founder and CEO of SAS, a giant, $3 billion, private software company. SAS sneaks under a lot of people's radar screens, but it's one of the most impressive stories in business. They develop business analytics software that helps companies do all sorts of things, like create targeted marketing campaigns, optimize supply chains, and manage risk.

Jim hires people who are off the charts on IQ, who are competent managers, and who share the values of the company. He invests a lot in them, and gives them plenty of second chances to succeed. He often does that by moving people around.

"Products are our people," Jim said. "It's a combination of the two when you work with people. You have to figure out what work group should be doing certain projects. Sometimes I have to move products around to different leaders and teams if the original team isn't getting it done."

Reorganization is sometimes the catalyst that funnels the right employees to the right spots and unleashes their best work. The Research and Development Division, for example, partnered with Human Resources last year in a large-scale effort to match employee strengths and goals with customer requirements.

So Jim keeps people on his team but moves them around to help them succeed.

That's right. He prides himself in keeping his people staffed on the right projects where they can perform as A Players. In fact, while he has had to let a few people go here and there, he has never had a layoff in nearly forty years. Today, SAS employs more than 13,000 people.

I think I've got the removing and moving parts down. You also mentioned hiring. How does that fit in?

If you don't have a full team of A Players who can achieve your priorities, you have to hire them.

Well, hiring is hard. It's just hit-or-miss, random chance, fifty-fifty, right?

True. The average hiring success rate is only 50 percent. You may be interested to know that nearly all full PWR leaders—69 percent of them—are great at hiring, which makes them more than five times more likely to be great at it than everybody else. Many of them follow the approach we describe in *Who* to achieve a 90 percent hiring success rate.

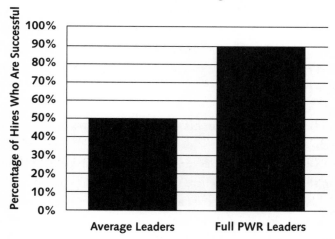

Typical Hiring Success Rates of Full PWR Leaders vs. Average Leaders

Source: ghSMART

Wow, a 90 percent hiring success rate?

Yes. You just have to avoid voodoo hiring and follow the *Who* method.

Voodoo *what*?

Voodoo hiring. It's using any approach to hiring that does not work.

For instance, do not ask candidates hypothetical questions such as "How would you fix this problem if you joined us?" We call this the Fortune-Teller approach, and it doesn't work.

Why not?

Because a half century of research in industrial psychology says that how people answer hypothetical questions is nothing like how they act in real life.

For example, I am going to ask you a hypothetical question. Say I'm interviewing you and say, "Here at my company, teamwork is really important. If you ever found yourself in conflict with a teammate, how would you resolve it?"

You want me to answer?

Yes.

Oh, well, I would resolve a conflict by first seeking out my teammate and scheduling a mutually convenient time to talk. I would never say bad things behind the person's back.

Of course not.

And I would sit down with my colleague and would say something like "Please tell me what is bothering you." Then I would

listen. After that, I would seek to resolve the conflict in a win-win way within a reasonable time frame.

Of course you would.

And then I would . . . Wait, I get it! When you ask someone a hypothetical question, you basically get a hypothetical answer!

Exactly. So don't ask people hypothetical questions in interviews. They tell you almost nothing about how the person will actually perform.

What are some other examples of voodoo hiring?

Another common one is being an Art Critic. That is when you make snap judgments on people—like critiquing a piece of art without any true expertise in the field. For example, you might be drawn in by someone with charisma while ignoring more reserved candidates.

Charisma is good, though, isn't it? I often hire charismatic, outgoing extroverts.

It can be good, although not necessarily. It depends entirely on the job. While not all charismatic leaders are extroverts, check this out. Thirty-three percent of all introverts we assessed turned out to be A Player leaders while 44 percent of extroverts were. And the success rate among the top 10 percent full PWR leaders was nearly identical between introverts and extroverts. While extroverts held a slight advantage in general, we cannot say that leadership favors one style over the other. Extroverts tend to "interview" better, but introverts perform just as well on the job.

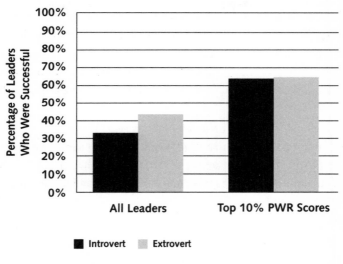

Success Rates by
Introversion and Extroversion

Note: n = 3,052 candidates
Source: ghSMART proprietary database

Wow, I never would have thought that. What are some other voodoo mistakes?

Talking during the whole interview is another voodoo hiring mistake. We often call those people Chatterboxes or Suitors because they either love to hear themselves talk or want to sell the candidate on the opportunity before they actually interview the person.

Thinking that your goal is to hire people you want to be stuck on airplanes with is a common mistake, too.

Wait a second, lots of people say you should *only* hire people you could tolerate for five hours of tarmac delays.

Yes, they do. But hiring managers overemphasize whether they like someone. And people tend to like people who are just like them. So hiring using the "Do I like them?" litmus test is both biased and unmeritocratic. We suggest you primarily evaluate whether they can do the job. Period. And if a person is a really great performer on the job, we believe you will like working with them!

So what am I trying to accomplish, if I hire well?

You are trying to hire an A Player. And you are trying to do this with as little expenditure of time and money as possible.

At ghSMART, we believe everyone is an A Player at something. Your challenge is to make sure the people you hire are A Players for the specific jobs you are filling, in your very specific company. If they are, then you can be 90 percent confident that they will achieve the results you want in the job.

So what are the steps of the *Who* method?

There are four steps to achieving a 90 percent hiring success rate: scorecard, source, select, and sell.

SCORECARD

The scorecard is the point where P (priorities) and W (who) intersect. You take your overall priorities for the team and then figure out how to assign specific outcomes to each person on the team. If people achieve the outcomes on their scorecards, your entire team should achieve its priorities.

It sounds a lot like the "what" of priorities.

Actually, it includes the why, what, and even the how, only broken down at an individual job level.

A scorecard answers three questions for each person's job in your company:

1. What is the mission for this role? (That's the why, as in "Why is this job important?")
2. What five to seven outcomes define what "A" performance means in this role? (That's the what, as in "What does the person in this role have to accomplish?") Recall from our conversation about priorities that outcomes are specific results that you can measure in terms of dollars, percents, numbers, and so on.
3. What competencies are especially important for this role? (That's the how, as in "How should this person behave?") Think of the skills and behaviors that define success in the role: persuasion, persistence, detail-orientation, organization, and so on.

When do I write the scorecard?

You'll want to write scorecards for your team right now and refresh them every year, or any time you reset priorities.

When you are hiring, write the scorecard *before* you start searching for candidates. That way, the people you meet in the recruiting process won't bias you.

After you do that, turn to the next step: source.

SOURCE

The source step is when you generate a flow of candidates. You can use recruiters, which is what most people do, or seek referrals from people you know. That's the better way, truthfully.

Start by making a list of the ten people in your network who you think will be the best referral sources. Then call them and ask, "Who do you know that I should consider hiring?" Tell them about the job, of course, so they give you targeted answers.

You can also offer an internal referral bounty to your team—$2,000, say, to any employee who refers a person that you hire.

I wish there were an easier way to source. Are you sure you aren't missing a silver bullet out there?

Unfortunately not. We have been asking leaders for years how they go about finding great people, and 77 percent of them say that getting referrals is by far the best route. You just have to have the discipline to keep at it. Consider yourself a perpetual chief recruiting officer.

That's what Kristin Russell called herself, in addition to her official designation as Colorado's former CIO. Kristin joined the state after a successful career at both Oracle and Sun Microsystems. When she had to bring new talent into her team, she was able to go out to the network that she had been building for years.

"Every single day, my job is to meet people and figure out how I can help them. I want to know what they are doing and what they are passionate about, and how I can align with them in their journey. Our paths might cross in the future, and having that network to draw upon as I've moved through my career has been critical. Because of that, I have been able to bring in some amazing talent."

Neat. So she is always recruiting. Everyone she meets could be a candidate or someone who knows others she should hire.
Exactly.

Once I get a good flow of candidates, I suppose I move on to the select step, right?
That's right. The select step is the hardest one.

SELECT

Hardest? Why?
Because it requires more discipline than many managers have when they interview candidates. But having the discipline to follow our four interview formats will help you achieve a 90 percent hiring success rate.

I've heard interviews don't work.
Some don't. A bunch of random questions rarely tells you anything useful. For example, asking people if they love to win or hate to lose might be fun for a party, but it doesn't help you when you are trying to make the most important decision you can make.

But good interviews are the most effective method for hiring.

What do I ask candidates the very first time I meet them or talk with them on the phone?

That is called the screening interview. It has four primary questions.

The Screening Interview

1. What are your career goals?
2. What are you really good at professionally? Please give me some examples.
3. What are you not good at or not interested in doing professionally? Please give me some examples.
4. Who were your last five bosses, and how will they each rate your performance on a 1-to-10 scale when we talk with them? Why?

Why do you start with career goals and motivations?

That goes back to what they really want. If their goals differ from what you need them to do, they won't be happy working for you. You will have a "will" mismatch in the skill-will bull's-eye.

Maynard Webb, the former president of eBay Technology and later chief operating officer, puts it well. He found restraining his eager-beaver employees a lot easier than having to motivate the ones who wouldn't get off the dime. As he described the work of making eBay scalable: "I knew I had to go to war, but was this the team I wanted to go to war with? I am a very simple man. If I have to run around every day and step on the gas for somebody who is only doing a piece of their job for me, well, that is a real problem. I would rather step on the brake and tell them we can't do it all at once but be thrilled that they want to do so much."

You want to find people who are passionately motivated to deliver your mission.

After that, compare their strengths and developmental areas with the rest of the job. If anything about them suggests they are not quite right, then screen them out. But if you are truly excited by the prospect of a great match, move on to the next step.

What's that?

That is when you wheel out the big gun, the Who Interview.

The Who Interview

The Who Interview is essentially a structured conversation in which you walk through people's careers in detail. You know you are doing it well when you learn a ton about a person as they tell you their career story.

First, to get things started, ask about their education. Ask them to tell you about high and low points for high school, university, and graduate school, spending about five minutes per school.

Then, walk chronologically through each job (or at least each job from the past fifteen years), spending twenty to thirty minutes per job and asking:

1. What were you hired to do?
2. What accomplishments are you most proud of?
3. What were some low points during that job?
4. Who were the people you worked with? Specifically:
    a. Bosses: What was your boss's name? How do you spell that? What was it like working with him/her? What will he/she say were your biggest strengths? Areas for improvement?
    b. Teams: How would you rate the team you inherited on an A, B, C scale? What changes did you make? Did you hire anybody? Fire anybody? How would you rate the team on an A, B, C scale when you left?
5. Why did you leave that job?

As they tell you their story, ask for lots of examples and get as concrete as you can by asking follow-up questions. The best questions are short and sweet, and begin with either a "what" or a "how." For example, what did you do? What were the results? How did you do it?

After working through each of their jobs, ask one last question: What are your career goals for the future?

You should already have a pretty good idea what the answer will be, but it's good to double-check.

What am I looking for as I listen to their career story?

Patterns that explain their successes and failures. What did they accomplish and how did they do it? What did they fail to accomplish and why? How well did they work with others?

How about an example to give me a better idea for how this works?

Sure, here's a true story about a candidate who wanted to become CEO of a company that was expanding into other geographic markets.

We started by asking him to tell us a bit about the highs and lows of high school, and he mentioned a paper route. Normally, we would not have spent much time on this, but something about the way he said it told us that maybe there was more to the story. Here's how it played out.

ghSMART: Tell me more about the paper route.

CANDIDATE: Well, I started the largest paper route in all of Michigan when I was fifteen years old.

ghSMART: How did you do that?

CANDIDATE: I analyzed the expected profitability of every neighborhood in my city. I found some huge apartment buildings that were easy to deliver to. Then I went and found the paper boy who delivered the papers to this area.

ghSMART: What happened?

CANDIDATE: I bought his route from him for two hundred dollars in cash.

ghSMART: What happened next?

CANDIDATE: I then started employing friends to deliver the papers. I stayed home and did the calculations of other paper routes I should buy. Then I looked at the customer acquisition costs and how to cross-sell papers. One summer I went on vacation for three weeks, and my team delivered tens of thousands of papers to our customers without a single mistake.

That is an amazing story!

It is, and it gets better. When we got to the candidate's first job and asked what he was proudest of accomplishing, he described how he had been the top salesperson by a long shot. Then, as we went to the next company and the one after that, he described how he had expanded sales in every case.

The industries differed but his methods were the same. They all traced back to how he had approached his paper route as a teenager. He had a very clear formula for his success.

That's what you are looking for—those patterns of success and failure. What makes someone successful? What causes them to fail? Once you find how someone has repeatedly succeeded and failed in the past, you can predict how they will help you in the future.

That seems pretty easy.

It's a very simple but powerful structure. We'll give you some more ninja tactics on how to execute it later in this section.

Great! But what about my other teammates? What interview questions should they ask candidates?

You know the scorecard by now—just carve it into pieces, hand them out to your three or four team members, and say, "I need you to interview this candidate on this part of the scorecard: _____." The blank is either a key outcome or a critical competency that you want to explore in more detail. This is called a focused interview.

Here's what your teammates would say to the candidate:

The Focused Interview

1. The purpose of this interview is to talk about _____ (one or more key outcomes or competencies from the scorecard).
2. What are some of the biggest accomplishments you have had in this area?
3. What are your biggest mistakes and lessons learned in this area?

After they interview the candidate, be sure to bring everybody together so you can compare notes and rate the scorecard together.

What about reference interviews? How do you get references to actually talk to you?

First, ask your candidate to introduce you to the people you want to call. That helps increase the chance you'll actually get to talk with them. Then make the reference interview broad to narrow. Like this:

The Reference Interview

1. In what context did you work with the person?
2. What were the person's biggest strengths? Please give me some examples.
3. What were some of the person's biggest areas for improvement back then? Please give me some examples.
4. How would you rate his/her overall performance in that job (1–10)?

5. The person mentioned that he/she struggled in that job with _____ (e.g., hitting deadlines, etc.); tell me more about that.

Wouldn't the reference give a biased report if the candidate set it up?

Maybe a little, but we have found that most references will give you good information if you follow this approach. Adding the words *back then* to the third question gives them permission to talk about the past, and presenting some areas the candidate mentioned as struggles often jogs their memory in a good way.

How do we decide whom to hire?

Once you do those interviews, assign A, B, and C ratings to the outcomes and competencies on the scorecard for each candidate. An "A" means you are 90 percent confident the candidate will succeed in that area. "B" means 50 percent. And "C" means less than 25 percent. If you have a candidate who averages an "A" or "A−"—*Boom!*—that's the one you want to hire.

Does it really work?

Oh yes. We regularly ask our clients to report how well it works for them. They track their progress, and typically improve their hiring success rates from 50 percent to 90 percent over time.

From half to almost whole—fantastic! But how do I get candidates to say yes?

That's the fourth and final step in hiring, which we call sell.

You definitely don't want to forget it after going through all of this work.

SELL

We asked more than one hundred successful leaders that we interviewed for *Who* how they sold their top candidates on taking the job. We grouped their responses into five categories that we call the Five F's of Selling:

1. Fit. This ties the company's vision, needs, and culture together with the candidate's goals, strengths, and values. "Here is where we are going as a company, and here is how you fit in."
2. Family. This takes into account the broader trauma to the family of changing jobs. "What can we do to make this change as easy as possible for your family?"
3. Freedom. This is the autonomy the candidate will have to make his or her own decisions. "I will give you ample freedom to make decisions, and I will not micromanage you."
4. Fortune. This reflects the stability of your company and overall financial upside. "Here's what you can make if you accomplish your objectives."
5. Fun. This describes the work environment and personal relationships the candidate will make. "I think you will find this culture one that you will really enjoy."

Basically, after you do the Who Interview, you will know what really matters to your candidate, and chances are high that it will include one or more of the Five F's. So build a closing plan that takes these things into account.

So, four S's to hire well—scorecard, source, select, and sell?
Yep. You got it.

Wait, you promised me some ninja tactics.
An overachiever, eh? Excellent! Here's a special bonus section with our best ninja tactics to help you sharpen your ability to hire the right who.

BONUS SECTION:
NINJA TACTICS OF INTERVIEWING

Intense Curiosity

I often wonder, "How should I act when I'm interviewing someone?"
Use a tone of intense curiosity.

Novice interviewers are often too stiff. They furrow their eyebrow and act very professional as if "I'm the boss and you are my subject." Or they are too casual.

None of these tones builds rapport as well as exuding intense curiosity. Candidates want to be understood. If you show you are interested in understanding them, they will tell you more information. And with more information, you have more data to help you determine whether they are a great fit to the job.

The easiest way to be curious is to ask many follow-up questions that begin with "what" or "how." What did you do? How did it go? What were the results? How did it feel? What . . . ? How . . . ? If you get stuck, just say, "Tell me more!" and your candidate will continue to share helpful details.

Get the Whole Story

What's another ninja tactic?

Listen for how people left their jobs. Were they pushed or pulled?

If they are constantly being *pushed* out of jobs, that is bad.

If they are being *pulled* to better jobs (by a customer or former boss who calls them out of the blue to rehire them, etc.), that is good.

Again, use your advanced interviewing skills to drill down until you discover the truth. Get the whole story. Too often, interviewers take the superficial top of a story at face value rather than digging in.

It's like mining for gold. Don't stop at mud and rock—go for the gold!

An example, please?

Sure. You be the judge of this one. We asked a CFO candidate why he left a job. He was a really nice guy and had fancy university degrees, both of which explain why he kept getting hired for jobs. But he was a chronic underperformer at CFO-level work. He told us he left a job "because I was reassigned."

In other words, pushed out?

Exactly. When someone gives you a vague answer like that, always, *always* follow up. We asked, "Reassigned to what?"

"Reassigned, to um, (swallow), to, um, Siberia."

What?! Surely that was a metaphor, right?

No, in this case it was literal: *Siberia!* His boss didn't have the heart to fire him. Instead, he reassigned the guy to Siberia, hoping he would take the hint and quit.

And he did.

No!

He went to Siberia?

Yes, for two years. The poor guy was miserable, and he failed at that job, too.

That's incredible that a candidate would tell you that.

People are willing to tell you more of the truth if you follow this method. In the end, we believe that everybody wins when the truth comes out. It allows you to deploy the right who to the right where, doing the right what. It's not good for anyone when people are in the wrong job—not good for the employer, not good for customers, not good for the employee himself.

Active Listening

Active listening, what's that?

The worst type of listening in an interview is when you talk the whole time. The next-best type of listening is to actually let them talk. A step above that, believe it or not, is repeating exactly what they say.

So a step above that, believe it or not, is repeating exactly what they say?

Ha, funny. Yes. But listen to this. The highest form of listening, the ninja tactic, is to reflect your understanding of the *emotion* behind their statement.

What do you mean?

Well, like this. If a candidate tells you that she had never built anything from scratch before and was sent to open a brand-new auto dealership in a new city with no support from her HQ location, you could just say, "So you were sent to open a brand-new auto dealership in a new city with no support from your HQ location." But that is not as good as saying something like this: "So you felt on your own." If she replies with something like "Exactly!" you know you have reached maximum rapport because you have connected on an emotional level. And when you have a high level of rapport, you are more likely to get the full story, the full truth, from a candidate.

When the Candidate Does Not Reveal Anything Negative

I hate it when candidates drone on about their positives, then clam up or fake it when I mention weaknesses.

Then stop asking people to tell you their weaknesses.

Instead, reframe the third question on "lows" in different ways until you hit on a question that resonates for them. Here are some examples:

1. What didn't go as well for you as you would have liked?
2. What was a meaningful mistake that you made?
3. What were some of your biggest lessons learned?
4. What did you dislike doing the most?
5. If you could do it all over again, what would you have done differently?

Another tactic is to use TORC (Threat of Reference Check). That is a term that Geoff's father, Brad, coined a few decades ago. Rather than asking people, "What are your weaknesses?" instead say, "We would like your help in setting up some reference interviews at some point, okay?" Candidates generally agree. Then you say, "When we talk with this person, what do you think he or she will say were your biggest strengths? Your biggest areas for improvement?" Knowing you're going to make the call, candidates will likely tell you quite a bit about their weaker areas.

Finally, you are actually doing reference interviews, so ask references. When references say, "I can't think of any weaknesses," you can offer the things the candidate guessed that the reference might say, and this sometimes primes the pump. Or, say to the reference, "You rated her an eight on a scale of one to ten. If she could have performed at the ten level, what would you have wanted her to do differently?"

That seems like an awful lot of work.

It is.

But think of the work it takes to deal with hiring people

into the wrong jobs. And think of the wrong you're doing not just to your team but to the mis-hire as well.

Yeah, it's probably good to take a little extra care in hiring right from the beginning.

That's what Tim Marquez found. He has a great rags-to-riches story, which he partly attributes to good hiring.

Tim grew up in a low-income household, but he didn't think it was all that bad. In fact, he told us that he remembers being quite happy when he was young. He was blessed with a close family and many friends from his tight-knit community who cared deeply about him. This gave him a clear sense for what truly mattered in life—using his talents to succeed professionally and to give back.

Tim attended public school in southwest Denver where graduation rates hovered around 50 percent. The word *college* never came out of anybody's mouth, and expectations were exceedingly low. With the encouragement of his parents, though, Tim studied hard anyway, and that set him up to continue his education. "My parents wouldn't have let me get away with anything else," he joked.

When he worked for an oil and gas company, he saw the importance of hiring and retaining great people—mostly by learning what not to do.

Tim said, "Unocal at that time said people were their most important asset, but it didn't mean anything. Good people were leaving, and every time a good person left, it became a marginally worse company. I got sick of working in its apathetic, directionless environment, so I decided to start something of my own. It wasn't about making money. I just like doing things the right way. You know, hiring well, treating people well, not cutting corners, and doing commonsense things."

Tim named his company Venoco. He started it with $3,000 as a one-man operation. He analyzed lists of oil fields and allocated his energy toward those that had the highest prospects. By the time he reached 1,000 barrels a day in production, he had the resources to make some key hires. Focusing squarely on the most important business needs, he hired an acquisition person to help identify properties, an engineer and geologist to do more technical work in the "down hole" side of things, and a land person to take care of all the leases.

Tim never lost sight of his commitment to hire well and treat people well. Those became mainstays of his leadership.

The approach worked. The company grew to some 450 people over the next few years, and from zero to over $1 billion.

Tim said, "I don't actually try to figure it all out myself anymore. I let them figure it out and make their recommendations. Sure, I have to adjust for one engineer being too conservative and another being too optimistic, but that is normal. I know that ten engineers will give ten different forecasts. My job is all about judging what they are recommending and then allocating resources. There's no magic other than getting really good employees and treating them really well. It is such a simple thing."

How about the "giving back" part? Did he take the money and run?

Not in the least. Tim's ability to get the who right enabled him to build a very successful company while pursuing a personal passion of his, education. He and his wife, Bernadette, launched the Denver Scholarship Foundation to support some of the poorest schools in Denver. The couple was able to write a check for $50 million to support the school system he attended.

Tim explained, "The reason graduation rates are so low in big cities like Denver is that kids can't afford to go to college, and if they aren't going to college, why should they finish high school? So we started with this idea of giving scholarships to kids to go to college. It also evolved to include putting Future Centers on school campuses. We run those like a business by hiring the right leadership team to do three things. They tell kids they can go to college, offer college counseling, and help with applications for scholarships and Pell Grants." Today, graduation rates and college enrollments are on the rise in Denver, and close to 3,000 Denver Scholarship Foundation scholars are in school right now thanks to Tim and Bernadette.

As he reflected on his rags-to-riches story, Tim told us, "You know, money is nice. What matters is what you do with it. I didn't give so much away because I am trying to earn points with anybody. It just makes me feel good to help people. Some of those kids are homeless or living out of a car. They are such good kids. They just need someone to care and to invest in their lives."

I think you're telling me that "who" has a multiplier effect that goes way beyond the workplace.

You got it.

DEVELOP

So we're done with the who stuff once we hire the person?

No. You still need to develop your team. Let's start with on-boarding, since great candidates can still fail if you don't take the time to settle them in and get them up to speed.

We suggest you follow this PWR framework:

1. *Priorities: discuss the scorecard.* On the first day of the job, have a ninety-minute conversation with your new hires to brief them on why you hired them and how the scorecard links back to the core priorities. This gets you on the same page, literally.

2. *Who: give development feedback from day one.* You've collected so much useful data about your hires through the interviews and reference checks that it just makes sense to use that for a debriefing. Tell your new hires what you think they will do well and where they will need to spend developmental energy to succeed in your organization. Help them build their first development plan, and support them as they execute it.

3. *Relationships: decide how and when to communicate.* Agree on a communication cadence up front. How and when are we going to communicate? Emails five times per day? Formal three-hour operating reviews quarterly? Setting a communication cadence is one of the easiest, most important, and least-practiced steps in on-boarding.

That second step is about development. How do I go about developing someone over time?

Develop your people's strengths by mapping them to roles that fit, mostly, and also try to play away from their weaknesses. Ask them, "What are your biggest strengths and how can we make them even stronger?" "What are any areas for improvement that are holding you back?"

That gets to the whole debate about focusing on people's strengths versus fixing their weaknesses. Where do you stand?

We believe that everyone should put two-thirds of their energy into building strengths. That is where you get the biggest bang for the buck, and it is more fun for your employees.

They still need to put one-third of their energy into being aware of, and managing, their weaknesses, though. You can't expect them to fix their weaknesses, but they may need to mitigate them so they don't derail their career.

How do we develop strengths and manage weaknesses? Training?

Training is a useful way to introduce new concepts, but here's a secret we've discovered by sifting through our data: Training accounts for only a small fraction of learning.

The majority of development comes through on-the-job experiences and the coaching you give people along the way. If you want people to grow, give them opportunities or assignments that play to their strengths while simultaneously stretching them. Then be there to support them.

How?

Set them up for success, for one. Remove roadblocks, introduce them to the right people, give them just enough direction to point them down the right path—those sorts of things. And when they have a problem, help them think through it without necessarily solving it for them.

Here is how Art Collins, the CEO of Medtronic, did it. He told us: "I am much more effective by asking questions rather than telling people what they ought to do, and the reasons are twofold. One, if you have smart people around you and you ask the right questions, they will come to the right answer on their own. And, two, once they come to that answer, it's not your answer, it's their answer, and they are going to be much more invested in actually taking it forward and successfully implementing whatever you decide."

That makes sense. Anything else?

Yes, one more thing, and it is really important. Debrief with your team often. After key meetings or calls, ask what went well, what didn't go as well, and what they would do differently. Most leaders neglect this critical step, but it makes a huge long-term difference in the careers of their reports because it forces them to reflect on what they are learning.

Speaking of careers, how do I help people manage theirs?

We suggest you encourage everyone on your team to build a career road map.

That's a long-term vision for how they want their career to go. We like to think of careers in stages. So to build a career road map, ask:

1. What are your long-term career goals?
2. What is the sequence of roles you want to play?
3. What do you want to accomplish this year?

Brad Smith, the CEO of Intuit, encourages his employees to have periodic conversations with their managers about their personal true north—the things that "make their heart beat fastest and where they most want to be." Then leaders work to match people to their polestars as much as possible. "It is not perfect, and we have to kind of maneuver," he said, "but it gets us a long way there."

Sum it up for me. How should I be thinking about the who on my team?

Go back to the first question: Do we have the right who? Specifically, do we have the right people matched to the right priorities? We call these Who-What pairings. Some call the process a talent review.

Every three months, sit down and ask yourself if you have the right people on your team. Measure the percentage of people who are achieving their outcomes, or who you think are likely to achieve their outcomes. You are shooting for 90 percent. That scores a 9 on the W.

As you think through your diagnosis, consider this question that an entrepreneur in one of our PWR Score workshops once offered: "If we were starting this company again today, would we want this person on the team or not?"

Once you complete your diagnosis, think through your plan to deploy your team. If people are falling short, your first instinct should be to ask the question "Are there roles in which these people can perform at the A level here?" If so, then move them. If not, then remove them from your team. Help them find jobs outside your organization that fit their particular skills and wills.

Finally, remember to support your team by on-boarding your new hires, developing their strengths while mitigating their weaknesses, and encouraging each of them to build a career road map that charts their future course.

Okay, I'm ready to rate our team on the W, from 1 to 10.

Go for it. Here are some hints about rating the W:

RATE THE WHO IN YOUR ORGANIZATION

"I think our W = _____ on a scale of 1 (low) to 10 (high)."

SCALE	DESCRIPTION	CHECK THE BOX THAT DESCRIBES YOUR WHO
1	"We have 0–10% A Players. Almost nobody here is in the right job. Several may be toxic to our culture."	☐
2	"We have 11–20% A Players. Very few are in the right job, and we have two or more people who are toxic to our culture."	☐
3	"We have 21–30% A Players. Some are in the right job, and we may have one or more people who are toxic to our culture."	☐
4	"We have 31–40% A Players. A third are in the right job, and we may have one or more people who are toxic to our culture."	☐
5	"We have 41–50% A Players. Nearly half are in the right job, and we may have one person who is toxic to our culture."	☐
6	"We have 51–60% A Players. Over half are in the right job, and we may have one person who is toxic to our culture."	☐
7	"We have 61–70% A Players. Most are in the right job, and nobody is toxic to our culture."	☐
8	"We have 71–80% A Players. Three-fourths are in the right job, and nobody is toxic to our culture."	☐
9	"We have 81–90% A Players. Almost everybody is in the right job, and nobody is toxic to our culture."	☐
10	"We have 100% A Players. Everybody here is in the right job, and everybody contributes positively to our culture."	☐

4

RELATIONSHIPS

Good news: The swimming and bike stages are done!

Bad news: Now I've got to run?
If you want to get to the finish line.

No sense coming this far and not going all the way. I've got P and W down, I think. What about relationships?
That's the R in the PWR Score. It is about getting relationships to work.

Sounds soft and fuzzy. Am I going to have to give my team a hug every morning?
We aren't talking about ambiguous touchy-feely relationships here. This is about building relationships that function well together and achieve results.

Full PWR leaders, those top 1 percent leaders who pull all three PWR levers, set incredibly high standards for their

teams and are over seven times more likely to hold them accountable to those standards versus all other leaders. And
they are two times more likely to follow through on their own
commitments than everybody else. There is nothing soft and
fuzzy about it.

So, they're serious about results.

You bet. Relationships are simply the way people behave
toward one another to achieve those results.

This is about ensuring that the members of your team take
coordinated action, commit to your cause, and constantly
challenge one another to achieve new heights.

And they get there when the leader cracks the whip?

Just the opposite, actually.

Leadership is about the relationship between a leader and
his or her followers. In fact, *relationship building* and *building
followership* are two of the most prevalent competencies found
in leaders who excel at the R. This is about them, not you.

Not only that, but great leaders know they must offset their
own weaknesses by building a strong team around them. Assuming they begin with the right who, building relationships
that work is about making the whole far greater than the sum
of the parts.

**This sounds like a way to amplify their individual effective-
ness.**

Precisely! As a leader, you derive your power from making
your team powerful. All progress in this world happens when

people pursue a worthy goal together. You may be their leader, but the team supplies the energy and does the work that leads to extraordinary outcomes.

Are you talking about *every* relationship in the whole organization?

Yes. Your immediate team, your boss, your peers in other departments, and teams across departments. They all count.

Think about a great conductor. He can't sit in all the sections or play all the instruments, but when he raises his baton at the start of a concert, he knows for sure that the strings and the horns and the percussionists know their parts and will blend into a beautiful symphony as soon as the baton comes down. What's more, and this is critical, he knows that *the musicians know* that the better they play their parts, the better the whole will sound.

A great conductor, a great baseball manager, a great schoolteacher, a full PWR leader—at the bottom line, they're all the same. They recognize that leading is about awakening the possibility within those they lead and helping them realize a vision bigger than themselves.*

What about *outside* the organization, like the relationships we have with key customers or suppliers or service providers?

Those, too.

---

* We first heard the phrase "awaken possibility in other people" in Benjamin Zander's remarkable TED Talk, "The Transformative Power of Classical Music." We highly recommend it.

"Relationships" include any relationship that matters to the success of your company. An orchestra depends on ticket vendors, lighting subcontractors, program printers, volunteer fund-raisers, even parking garage attendants to do their job as well. If they're not on board, orchestras suffer no matter how well they play.

The point is to figure out whether or not relationships inside or outside the organization are working. If they are, then keep doing what you are doing. If they're not, pinpoint the weak links and do something different to make them work better.

Where do I begin?

Start by thinking about the previous two sections. Do you have the right priorities and the right who? Many leaders miss these steps and go straight into fixing relationships, not realizing they have ambiguous priorities or weak players on their team. That's backward. If you sense something is wrong with your relationships, double-check your priorities and who first.

Once you get those right, ask yourself three questions to see how close to a 10 you score on relationships that work:

- Is communication *coordinated* within and beyond the team?
- Is our team *committed* to the mission and to one another?
- Does our team feel *challenged* to accomplish something bigger than themselves?

Seek to build teams that are:

- COORDINATED
- COMMITTED
- CHALLENGED

COORDINATED

Coordinated. Is that like clarifying roles and responsibilities?

Sort of, but that's not the complete story. It has more to do with aligning people around the same priorities and ensuring the right information flows between them. "Coordinated" is about getting people together and tracking progress against goals.

The scorecard can be quite powerful here. It's a terrific way to capture priorities—for both your team and the individuals on your team. If you write the scorecard well, the outcomes section will include key goals.

Now, you need to bring the right people together in the right communication cadences to talk about your priorities and track progress against the key goals.

"Communication cadences" sounds interesting, but help me understand how it works.

"Communication cadences" is making sure the right people are communicating with one another at the right times. This could be through meetings, calls, and even shared experiences.

Failure to communicate sufficiently is one of the biggest
points of feedback people receive when we give them a 360 assessment. It usually happens because they have no formal system in place to force the right conversations to happen. Other
times, the problem reflects a failure to share critical information at the right moments or to involve all the right people at
the right times to solve problems.

To fix this, ask yourself these questions:

- Are the right people communicating at the right times?
- Are the right people getting the reports, metrics, and
  dashboards they need to make good decisions?
- Are the right people coming together to solve the right
  types of problems?

How do the 9's and 10's do this?

Verne Harnish of Gazelles does it through a weekly huddle.
His team is truly global. "They are all independent entrepreneurs from across twelve and a half time zones around the
world who come together to help Gazelles," Verne said. "Our
Monday morning huddle lets us tackle the big issues and challenges for the week."

The first thing he does during these calls is check in with
everybody. Rome may be burning, but they still take a moment to go around and share a piece of good news personally
and professionally with one another.

Wouldn't that take a lot of time away from a critical meeting?

To the contrary, it helps bring everybody together. As Verne
said, "Leadership is really about connecting with people as

human beings and not as inputs into a managerial process. The check-in is really critical."

After the check-in, they discuss, debate, and decide on two or three big topics. "We don't put off specific decisions that need to be made. If we want to move faster, we need to pulse faster."

Discuss, debate, decide. I like that.

You can use it if you want. We call it 3D at ghSMART—as in, "Let's 3D this issue."

Anyway, at the end of Verne's meetings, everyone gets a chance to check out with a concluding remark, and then they review the next steps. "It's not micromanagement," Verne said. "It is great management."

I like the huddle, but how do I keep my meetings from devolving into boring status updates?

Atul Gawande's management meetings were typical progress updates. His team showed up, and they took turns to share where their projects were ahead, on track, or behind. Atul would help problem-solve if needed, but everyone was bored out of their minds, including Atul.

Interesting discussions rarely happened. Atul considered getting rid of the meeting altogether. It would have been a popular decision initially, but it also meant that projects might slip and the teams would be unaware of their overlaps.

Instead, Atul and his team decided to blow up the agenda. Rather than share project status, everyone now has to submit a tough question they are grappling with and their recommended solution. The meetings transformed almost overnight from boring status reports to engaging problem-solving sessions.

"Now we have to prepare for meetings," one of his teammates told us, "but it is worth it." One subtle shift in the agenda transformed the entire thing.

What about some other ways to coordinate?

It's worth focusing on Atul for a moment longer because he popularized an incredibly important way to coordinate people, which he outlines in his book *The Checklist Manifesto.*

Atul discovered that the simple act of putting key actions into a checklist ensured that the right people had the right conversations at the right times. It's a universal best practice of leadership across many industries, from medicine to airlines to investing to hiring.

For example, Atul described how asking some simple questions before an operation starts—such as "Have all team members introduced themselves by name and role?" "How much blood loss should the team be prepared for?" and even "Have we checked the patient's ID bracelet to make sure we are about to operate on the right person?"—can reduce complications and deaths by more than a third.

Weekly problem-solving huddles and running through checklists strike me as good hygiene practices. What can I do to take this to the next level?

Many leaders take it a step further by creating shared experiences for their team. This pushes people beyond talk and into action.

Scott Cook, founder of Intuit, discovered that shared experiences align people very quickly around a common set of priorities. "People learn by doing," he said. "When people end up with different points of views, it is usually because they have had different experiences. If you want them to come to the same point of view, you need them to share the same, or nearly the same, experiences first. For example, our leaders in our TurboTax division have taken everybody out to see customers on the same day and then come back to debrief together." Their debriefs may be spirited, but they start from the same baseline.

Scott continued, "I don't think you align a team by talking about it or issuing orders. I think you align by helping them believe in what you are doing, and you do that by giving them the same, shared experience."

So getting people coordinated is about getting them together one way or another to focus on the highest priorities. What's the right cadence for this?

Generally, teams we see follow different cadences for different topics:

- Every ten years to revisit the mission, vision, and values.
- Every three years to revisit the strategy.
- Every year to create the annual plan and scorecards.
- Every quarter for reviewing goals versus results.
- Every month to review progress.
- Every week or even day to work out problems.

The every-quarter and every-month cadences bring us to an important aspect of coordinated teams: dashboards and metrics. You have to make sure people know how they are doing versus their goals.

Take FedEx, for example. Its famous Purple Promise is about making every FedEx experience outstanding. It's a great goal, but how do you get more than 300,000 team members to fulfill it every single day?

Dashboards and metrics?

Bingo. CEO Fred Smith cut his teeth in the Marines during two tours of duty in Vietnam. He paid very close attention to how the military thought about logistics and leadership. As he built the "absolutely, positively" culture at FedEx, he realized that dashboards reflecting operational performance and metrics tied to compensation would ensure that everybody focused on the right things. "For senior leadership, 80 percent of the compensation is tied to company results and 20 percent is tied to individual results," he told us. "For frontline folks, nearly all of their compensation comes from their individual results." You can bet his team pays close attention to performance dashboards and key metrics.

But what about a small entrepreneurial shop? A place like that doesn't need all that big-company bureaucracy.

Setting goals and following up is not bureaucracy. It's a discipline that you need to practice if you want to run at full power. Staying coordinated is important. "What gets measured gets done," as the saying goes.

Do I have this right so far? Coordinating relationships means getting the right people to talk to one another about the right things at the right times, and tracking progress as they go.

Right again. Relationships work much better when everybody is rowing in the same direction. Tracking progress through communication cadences and measuring it with metrics keep everybody coordinated, aligned, and working toward the same goals. It makes it far easier to hold everybody accountable to their individual parts of the big picture, and it ensures that your team tackles the right problems.

However, coordinated relationships are just table stakes when it comes to building high-powered teams. You need to tap into something more intrinsically visceral to truly drive results.

That is where committed relationships come in.

COMMITTED

Commitment sounds scary. Why does it matter so much?

The best strategy in the world won't work if your people aren't committed. They won't make things happen unless they feel emotionally invested in their work.

That makes commitment the fuel that powers your team. It inspires people to be more. It motivates them to do more.

A small group of committed teammates makes all the difference.

What must my team commit to, exactly?

To your mission, to you as their leader, and to one another. You need all three to truly shine.

Okay, so I start with my mission. This sounds like revisiting my priorities.

That's right, only now you need your team to buy into them, and specifically to the overarching mission. Your mission must jump off the page and come alive within your team. Otherwise, they'll struggle to find their way on their own.

Razor Suleman nearly failed as an entrepreneur for this exact reason. He kept his dreams bottled up inside his own head rather than sharing them, and it nearly destroyed his company.

Back in 2006, he told us, he found himself stumbling along the beach with tears in his eyes, thinking about taking another job or becoming a bartender for a while rather than continue on with the company he had started. He was struggling as a founder entrepreneur, and six of his eighteen-person leadership team had just resigned in exasperation. It was his fault, and he knew it—it wasn't supposed to be like this. When he was younger, Razor had had a vision of building a software company to change how organizations work. It was so clear to him. He saw the opportunity to build enterprise software that helped companies engage and retain their employees. Ironically, his employees were leaving in droves.

"I was failing as a leader and as an entrepreneur," he said. "I was not providing a great place to work or communicating the vision of the company to the team. People were running out the door, and I was right behind them."

Sounds like reality was crashing all around him.

Was it ever. Razor went into his COO David Brennan's office one day and threw his keys onto his desk. "I've had it," he told him. "I quit. It is done. I am not good at this."

That could have been Razor's final act, but David didn't let him off the hook. "Here's the problem," David said. "You have this movie in your head, but only you see it. You don't tell anybody about it. You need to write it down and communicate it to the entire company. Expose all the things you are thinking about how the world should work and then let's review that."

Razor was skeptical at first and spent that first evening looking into bartending jobs. Despite his doubts, he got more serious on the second night and started to write. In only fifteen minutes, he created five pages of handwritten notes about his dreams. He described the company he wanted to build and the customers he wanted to serve. He described the kind of employees he wanted to hire and how he would engage with them. And he described his values and how they would become the values of the company. Most implausibly, he wrote down his financial goal to reach $1 billion in sales over the next five years. Putting all of this to paper was liberating and a far cry from serving drinks on a beach.

The next morning, Razor presented his five-page manifesto to his COO with a certain amount of trepidation. "This is great," David told Razor. "This is big. Now you need to share it with the team at the off-site later this month."

Razor's heart sank. "They'll think this is crazy!"

"They will think your vision is crazy," David replied with a smile. "In fact, they might think you are crazy, but you have to put it out there. That's what leaders do."

Razor delivered his vision to the employees in an all-hands meeting in 2006, and two more executives resigned the very next day. It reinforced Razor's worst fears: They really did think he was crazy.

I'm doing this on the back of a napkin. But that makes eight of eighteen who bailed, right? Nearly 45 percent of his team?

Right, but then it struck Razor: While eight had quit, ten had stayed!

"The ten people who stayed *got it*," he told us. "They believed. They saw a better world and believed we had the potential to go there. I wanted to take this to the moon but had nothing to offer them that proved we could do it. All I had was a belief and the enthusiasm and passion to get there. They decided to stick with me to see if we could get to the moon or crash in the effort."

The team began to hire against Razor's vision and mission by sharing it with everybody they interviewed.

"If candidates didn't like the vision, that was okay," Razor said. "It was self-selection. Why would I want to pay people who didn't want to go where we were going?"

Over time, the team that remained and the team they hired became full converts to the vision. Some still thought Razor was slightly crazy, or at least overly ambitious, but there was something infectiously exciting about that. They wanted to be in business with him. They wanted to take a shot at going to the moon with him.

And to the moon they went. The team framed Razor's five-page manifesto, which he calls his MasterPlan, and hung it on the company wall, where it remains to this day. On the basis of that MasterPlan, his company, Achievers, raised $38 million, led by Sequoia Capital in its early days, and has passed its first $100 million in sales after doubling every year in the last six years. Achievers has also been recognized as a Top 100 Employer in each of the past six years. In addition, it was the fastest-growing company in North America when Razor won the Ernst & Young Entrepreneur of the Year Award in 2011. Today, the company serves employees in 110 countries around the world, boasts a 99 percent customer retention rate, and most important, delivers on their mission: To Change the Way the World Works.

So he wasn't just another dreamer who couldn't deliver?

Far from it. As Razor put it: "When I described my vision in 2006, people thought I was delusional. Today, it almost feels like our vision is small. It is in sight. I learn from my failures, and in this case, I learned that it is important to create the vision, set the direction, and communicate, communicate, communicate." No wonder he proudly carries the title: Founder, Chairman, and Chief Achiever.

Knowing who you are and what you stand for is important, but it is not enough. You also have to share where you are going so others can decide if they want to follow you or not. Sure, you might seem a little like a nutcase, but the right fit in any job situation goes far beyond academic credentials and even past experience.

Doesn't this get back to the idea of the skill-will bull's-eye that we discussed in the Who section?

Basically, it's the same thing, but there we focused on a

decision—does someone have the will or not? Here, we focus on what you need to do as your team's leader to engender commitment to the mission.

How else can I create commitment to my cause?

Kent Thiry, CEO of DaVita, walks across a special bridge every morning on the way to his office.

What, like on his commute?

No, this bridge isn't even outside. It is a ten-foot wooden hump with railings that sits out in an open area near Kent's office inside DaVita's Denver headquarters.

We walked across it, just to see what all the fuss was about. It's really not that exciting an experience. What matters to Kent and his team is what crossing the bridge represents.

Kent crosses it every day not only to set an example to others about his steadfast and unwavering commitment, but also to remind himself of the high aspirations he has for this unique and special community—*not* company.

What do you mean? What's the big deal?

The big deal is purpose. Kent is on a mission that is more than just making money and bigger than just building a company. He views his role as building a community.

This sounds a little on the edge. Cue the eerie music?

Keep listening. It gets weirder and more intriguing.

By walking across the bridge, Kent recommits every day to the mission and values of the company. Kent's title is "Mayor."

And his employees are called "teammates" or "citizens" of the "Village."

This is a public company?

Yes. It was called Total Renal Care when Kent first joined in 1999, and it was in the pits—nearly bankrupt. The Securities and Exchange Commission was investigating the company, shareholders were suing it, and about half the senior leadership team had either been terminated or were in the process of jumping ship. Those who remained were unable to track critical financial or clinical outcomes, but everybody knew that the numbers were bad. Turnover was in the high 30s. People were angry, scared, and completely demoralized.

Kent was scared, too. He had no idea if he could fix this desperately broken company. To make matters worse, he knew even trying would come at a very high personal cost. He and his family lived in San Francisco, but the company was based in Los Angeles.

At the same time, Kent was very excited. He had a dream about building a company that truly made a difference in the world. This felt like an opportunity to fulfill that dream. After a rather spirited discussion with his family, he finally won their support and took the job.

When he first arrived, Kent decided that the single most important thing he could do as a leader was give his team hope. He knew he couldn't make any progress until they once again believed in the company.

So, he asked them to commit to the company?

No, not at first. Instead, he shared his personal dream. "I said it out loud. I said I wanted to create a special place to work. I wanted to build the greatest dialysis company the world had ever seen."

Some people embraced Kent's pronouncement, but even more people rejected it. "A third of the people in the room were downright hostile in their reaction. A third were indifferent and thought it was just rhetoric. Only a third said, 'Yeah, that would be cool.' It was very uncomfortable, but I still felt like it was the right thing to do."

Kent's dream triggered a host of questions, but most of them boiled down to one: How are you going to do that?

Rather than dismiss the questions or offer half-baked answers, Kent gave them a surprising reply. "I am dedicated to this dream, but I don't have a master plan," he told them.

"We are going to create the plan together. And it will be about a company that adds value to people's lives and helps people realize their full potential."

Ah, I get it! He put the task of creating priorities on his team. That is a great way to commit people to the cause.

Yes, and it enabled him to build momentum. As the initial months rolled by, people started to see what kind of company it would be and what Kent was trying to do. People responded by asking for a new name for this new company.

Kent took this democratic request to heart and asked his team to propose new names to vote on along with the old ones. The name DaVita was born, which roughly translates to "giving life."

Is that common, for employees to vote on a company's name change?

There could be others, but it's the only Fortune 500 company we have heard of that threw the question open to all its employees.

The name change didn't make much of a dent in the culture, though. Over the course of the next year, Kent spent countless hours on the road, holed up in dingy hotel conference rooms with groups of DaVita employees. "I would talk about my hopes and look out at the people and see they were just totally dead. At night, alone in those hotel rooms and far away from my family, I would say to myself, 'This isn't working, and I am looking kind of foolish!' There were many times when I wanted to give up. I recall one time when I went up to my room and cried, which happened out of a combination of sheer exhaustion and frustration as I crisscrossed the country promoting this vision.

"Then a beautiful thing happened. One of our really seasoned operators, a quiet sixty-year-old woman who had said virtually nothing for the first four months I was there, came over and sat down next to me at one of these events. She put her hand on my knee and said, 'Kent, you are trying to do the right stuff. I am on board.' That gave me the energy to continue."

As Kent went about engaging people from all parts of the company, he started asking them how people behaved on a healthy team. "Everybody could answer that question whether they had been to college or not. Everybody wanted to be part of a special team or a special community."

Okay, so here's where the community idea comes in.

That word kept coming up, Kent told us: *community*. "One night I said, 'Okay, we are going to be a community first and a company second because that is what people want. People in a community care about one another and care about the community overall, so let's be that.'" Soon DaVita employees were calling themselves citizens of their village and referring to Kent as Mayor KT—short for Mayor Kent Thiry.

Did his board of directors think this was a good idea, or just weird?

No doubt about it: just weird. "When I first told the board about this," Kent said, "they thought I had lost my sanity and was completely off my rocker. They worried that we wouldn't pay enough attention to performance standards and operating metrics. If you think about it, though, the mayor of a village first has to build a stable economy and instill confidence, because otherwise you cannot do any good for your citizens. A mayor doesn't go home and brag about his or her GNP. A mayor goes home and proudly talks about the community's schools, parks, absence of crime, and degrees of citizenship. For us, profit is a means to the end, not *the* end. However, we knew that building a community would take time and that positive results would not be immediate. We needed latitude from our board to realize this vision. We let them know that if latitude was not provided, we would move on to something else."

With many skeptics still in the company, Kent decided to make the message very real and very tangible by making crossing the bridge more than just a figure of speech.

So he built an actual bridge and had people walk across it?

You got it. "We called a second special nationwide meeting and put three bridges in the room," he told us. "I was standing in front of thousands of DaVita citizens and I said, 'We've now spent months and months talking about this stuff. Do you believe in this mission and values? Do you believe in the notion of community first and company second? If so, it is time to cross the bridge. You don't have to do it publicly or in front of anybody. At some point in the next two and a half days, we want every person in this room to cross the bridge—or not. If you can't, then all we ask is that you take some time for some serious personal and professional reflection, and if you still can't reach a decision, then ask yourself if this is the right career fit.

"Thousands of people did cross the bridge and became citizens of our village by their own admission."

As Kent has reflected on his experience, he has come to believe that his job as a leader boils down to the simple task of unleashing human potential. "I believe that ninety-eight percent of the people in this world just want to be part of a good team doing good work that does good for the world. My job is to liberate them from these old ways of doing things and unleash their own basic desires."

Meanwhile, DaVita's stock was the top S&P 500 performer from 1999 to 2012. Far better, countless customer lives have been improved by tens of thousands of DaVita citizens who want to make a difference in the world and, thanks to Kent's leadership, are succeeding.

You mentioned commitment must extend beyond the mission to the leader and even the team. How does that work?

Let's start with the leader. Even if people buy into the mission of your organization, they will struggle mightily if they don't believe in you as their leader. You have to earn their trust by becoming a leader worth following.

Randy led a sales team at a software company prior to joining ghSMART. He thought he was doing a good job until a sales manager came to him one day and said, "You know what? It doesn't always feel like you are out front with your sword outstretched, encouraging us to take the hill." It was one of the lowest moments in Randy's career, but also a tremendous learning opportunity.

Randy had been tracking progress carefully through one-on-one status meetings with his sales team and extensive dashboards and metrics, so this was not a question of whether or not the team was coordinated. The problem revolved around his failure to spend enough time in the field to help his team win new business. He was administering just fine, but he was leading his sales team from the rear.

"Am I leading by example? Do I walk the talk?" Those are questions we all need to ask ourselves, but witness Randy: you also need to involve your team to get a really honest read. Randy thought he was doing fine, but his team felt otherwise.

So, it's about being genuine and honest with yourself?

That's where building commitment starts, certainly. Plus, you need to role-model the behaviors you want to see.

If you preach respect, are you acting respectfully toward

everyone, or do you show up late for meetings and neglect to listen to people?

If you preach innovation, have you created an environment where innovation can happen, or do you ridicule people whenever they try something new?

If you say you want a collaborative team environment, are you doing everything you can to achieve it, or do you work in a vacuum and assume others will collaborate around you?

Role modeling is hard, but it is foundational to your ability to build relationships that work.

Why is role modeling so hard?

Because it takes courage. Sometimes leaders just chicken out on doing the right thing in favor of going with the flow.

Sometimes you have to stand up for your colleagues, to show them that you have their back. That is what Joyce Russell did. She runs Adecco Staffing US, a $2.8 billion division of Adecco Group North America. The company provides temporary and contract staffing, permanent recruiting, and managed services to its clients around the world.

Early in her career, Joyce's business line incurred a one-time unusual financial item that affected Adecco's financial performance for that period. Many of Joyce's senior leaders would be negatively impacted on their financial results, even though they had no involvement in the specific incident.

"We had one leader who ran a major metropolitan market for us. Over the years, this colleague had contributed millions of dollars to the organization. Our senior leadership was making the case that everybody should be included in the group that would take the financial hit. I strongly disagreed since this individual had not been involved, and I thought it would be unfair to include this colleague in the group."

Standing up to her CEO took courage and conviction. He was an impressive leader with strong convictions of his own built on years of experience. Joyce said, "I could see from his body language that he strongly disagreed with the position I was taking. Then he told me a story about something very similar that happened to him earlier in his career. He said, 'Sometimes, Joyce, that is just the way it goes.'"

Gut-check time.

Sure was. Joyce told us she could feel her pulse quicken. The blood rushed to her head as she built up the nerve to defend her position. Finally, she leaned forward in her chair and looked her CEO directly in the eye. "You know what?" she said to him. "We are the leaders now, so we get to make those decisions—we get to decide. We need to make sure this doesn't happen under our leadership. We need to make sure that we don't pass on poor leadership decisions."

Her CEO paused. Everybody in the room was quiet. Nobody came to her defense. Finally, the CEO went around the room to see what everybody thought, and all that could be heard were crickets.

Then he turned back to Joyce and said, "You are right."

The CEO continued as Joyce exhaled. "I have never been more proud of you than at this moment." Turning back to the group, he said, "You know what, everyone, she is right, and I am wrong."

"I will never forget that moment," Joyce said.

She won the debate.

She did, but that was far from the end of it. As Joyce told us: "That colleague is still with the company, and I can guarantee this person wouldn't be here if we hadn't done the right thing. It would have been a terrible loss had that colleague left. On top of that, my CEO promoted me from chief operating officer to president of the company a few months later.

"When I think about leadership, I think about the personal courage you have to have to stand up for what is right and what you believe in, even if it's unpopular or a political land mine. That is particularly true with your people. You have got to stand up for your people, to have their back."

What are other examples of great role modeling?

Following through on your commitments turns out to be extremely important. Your team will never respect you if you ignore the promises you make.

Bill Amelio said it well. "When you make commitments, you need to keep them. That is the best way to build trust and credibility. It is the little things. If I say I am going to give you a raise on such and such day and that actually happens, then I build trust and credibility. Or if I tell you I am going to remove an obstacle that is in your way and I actually get it done, then that builds a lot of trust and confidence in your leadership."

Communicating transparently builds trust, too, not only in you as the leader, but also in your whole organization.

Most leaders work hard to control the information that flows about their organization, often to the point of hiding things they don't want others to know. Think about how many scandals would have been averted, or at least mitigated, if the leader had just told the truth from the beginning.

We have met some leaders who take the exact opposite approach. They share everything—the good and the bad—every day. They publish their financials, offer direct feedback, publish ratings scales, and shoot straight rather than spinning the story. People always know exactly where they stand and how they will be treated.

People joining their teams find the transparent culture jarring at first, but they soon realize they can count on their leader and the organization to operate fairly because everything is out in the open. These leaders leave no room for bad behaviors, and their teams quickly learn to trust them.

"Trust" keeps showing up in these stories.

For good reason: *Trust* is the key word. People will commit their time and energy to you if they trust you. The opposite happens if they don't trust you. They won't follow you, and then you will never have the commitment you need to build strong and powerful relationships. Trust makes or breaks a team, and it starts with your being trustworthy. You can't empower your team members otherwise, and if you can't do that, you'll never get where you want to be.

Enlightened self-interest then?

In part, for sure, but if you've got relationships that work, there's no difference between your interests and those of your team—or your company or your customers or society as a whole, for that matter. Everyone wants to succeed, but it all begins with mutual trust.

Okay, fine, but how do you build trust? Do you have a checklist for that?

You bet. Here's a starter list, although it could be much longer:

- Be a person of character. Always maintain ironclad honesty and integrity. Be consistent in everything you do.
- Operate authentically.
- Lead by example.
- Work as hard as your team. Be willing to get your hands dirty.
- Get things done. People like to be on a team that wins.
- Follow through on your commitments.
- Communicate transparently, directly, and clearly.
- Listen intently and sincerely.
- Support your team rather than looking out for yourself.
- Demonstrate care and compassion.
- Defend your team, particularly when they are absent from the room.
- Give credit and accept blame.
- Be generous.
- Resolve conflicts.
- Remove roadblocks.
- Live the values.

I noticed you listed integrity first. Some say that is the key to all of leadership.

It is certainly important, but don't fall into the trap of

thinking that it is the only thing. Ninety-one percent of everybody in our database had unquestionable integrity, but only a fraction of them were effective leaders. Being a person of character is a minimum requirement, but it doesn't guarantee your success.

Of course, lacking integrity will hurt you because every little thing you do either builds or erodes trust with your team. Every word, every action, every move you make. To become a leader worth following, show people you care and have their best interests at heart. Model the behaviors that build trust. Only then will they commit themselves to you.

Not only that, but encourage your team to do the same. Ultimately, they need to commit to one another just as much, if not more, than they commit to you.

How do you set up a team to commit to one another?

Caperton Flood, a partner at Bain & Company, offers a great example. He consistently has teams that go above and beyond for him. Not only that, but his teams tend to go above and beyond for one another, too. Despite long hours and hard work, they are amazingly loyal.

Growing up in Kentucky gave Caperton a lilting southern accent and an easygoing, approachable style, but those alone aren't the secret to his success.

When he kicks off a project, he brings his team together to describe the deliverables and timeline. Like most projects at Bain, Caperton's tend to involve fast-paced mergers-and-acquisitions deals or urgent competitive strategy situations. After running through one such project plan, Caperton pulled out a blank piece of paper. "What, if anything, are we prepared to commit to one another on this project?" he asked. The team mostly stared at the floor and shuffled uncomfortably in their seats. Caperton sat quietly.

Slowly, one by one, people began to speak up. "Well, I really want to keep my weekends free, but I am happy to put in long hours during the week to make that work," one said.

"But what if the client calls us on a Friday at three P.M. and asks for something by Monday A.M.?" he pressed.

"Perhaps we could check our email at eight P.M. before switching off for the night, and again at eight A.M. to check in the next morning," one person offered.

"Maybe we could each pick a night to protect for family or personal matters," another chimed in. The discussion continued for another twenty minutes, and soon Caperton had documented a list of commitments.

He passed the paper around the room, and every member of the team signed it.

Twenty minutes to get a commitment, eh? Not bad.

He got an explicit commitment, yes, but people can be fickle, particularly as time passes or when they are under pressure. No matter how committed they may feel to the mission, to you as their leader, or to their team, time and stress have a funny way of eroding those commitments and diminishing their resolve.

To offset the diffusion of commitment, continuously remind your team why they committed in the first place.

How about through repeated communication?

Absolutely. The more you communicate a message, the

more your team will remember why they are there and understand what you want them to do.

"People need to hear things five to six times," one leader told us. "I probably communicated my messages only three to four times. I didn't follow through. Not just laterally, but all the way down. I find I am at my best when I communicate more. I am at my worst when I default to doing the work alone rather than engaging others and letting them know what is going on."

Is saying something five or six times really enough?

No, not even close. Meaningful communication requires countless repetitions. It takes discipline, which is probably why most leaders undercommunicate by a long shot. Not Jim Donald, though. The CEO of Extended Stay Hotels shows us that you can go a lot further than most of us imagine. Jim sends a sixty-second voice mail to every employee.

Every.

Single.

Day.

Jim has been sending out a daily voice mail for twenty-two years. Think about that! Allowing for weekends, that is some 5,700 messages. Those messages have been heard tens of millions of times across the tens of thousands of people in his companies.

The messages are clear and simple, and it doesn't take long before people start to understand his intent. "To get aligned," he said, "you have to make sure you get in front of everybody. That is why I do it by voice mail. They hear my voice. I am in their living room every single day. It builds trust."

That's lot of voice mails! I've got a sore throat just thinking about it.

It is, but you don't have to do it that way. You could send out weekly emails or host monthly town hall meetings with everybody on your team. There are loads of ways to communicate. The key is to keep it up because reinforcing the right behaviors takes constant vigilance.

We have found that you need to communicate something at least twenty times before people really start to tune in to it. You'll get way beyond the point where you can't stand to hear yourself say it again, but do it anyway. Keep communicating until you know your team has heard you, and then say it again and again to reinforce the message.

What about rewarding people to reinforce their commitment? How do you think about that?

Most people go straight to financial rewards, and those matter. But consider recognizing and rewarding people in other ways, too.

For example, when Eric Foss became CEO of Pepsi Bottling Group, he announced he wanted to create a culture of appreciation. He was very clear about the behavior he wanted to reinforce, but how should he do it?

His chief human resource officer at the time, John Berisford, put it into action based on some experience he had had. "When someone writes me a note, I keep the card," John said. "But I don't keep an email. I developed an idea. We had a leadership meeting, and I delivered a speech to explain my theory. I got stationery for each leader. It even had their name on top. I said we weren't going to inch our way into this culture of appreciation. Over the next thirty minutes, we were going to write thank-you notes for everyone who we should have thanked in the last year. We mailed several thousand that day. Over the next year, employee engagement went up 26 percent. The stock price went from twenty-three dollars to eighty-two dollars over the ten years that Pepsi Bottling Group was a public company."

How can you know that the thank-you notes improved employee engagement? For that matter, how do we know that employee engagement drove company results?

The notes were just one aspect of Eric and John's plan to reinforce the culture. They took other actions, too, that drove performance.

As for engagement driving results, Gallup has done a lot of research on that. CEO Jim Clifton told us, "The link between employee relationships and financial performance has never been more clear." He went on to show us study after study that link the two. Engagement correlates with results—you can count on it.

Not only that, but Jim practices what he preaches, and Gallup's stock has gone from $15 in 1988 to $825 per share today.

Where does compensation factor in? Doesn't that have a lot to do with what motivates people to stay engaged?

There's legitimate debate about whether people are more motivated by intrinsic things, like the thrill of doing a task, or by extrinsic things, like how you financially reward them.

We think that both matter. Recognizing people for the great

work they do is intuitively satisfying, as we have already discussed. Paying them well makes them happy, too, although it tends not to motivate them for long.

Really? I would have thought compensation was a big deal.

It is if you don't pay people enough. Compensation is funny that way. Its upside is short-lived, but underpaying will certainly demotivate someone. It becomes like a thorn in their side.

Assuming you pay enough, the true value of compensation is aligning incentives to your goals. Otherwise people sense the disconnect or begin to behave in strange ways.

For example, there was a time when lawyers were paid by the word. Guess what they did? They wrote exhaustive briefs and contracts! That wasn't in the best interest of the client.

We have worked with many sales teams that struggle with similar problems. They compensate based on revenue, but the company really cares about margins. Or maybe they launch a new product but neglect to put any incentives in place to promote it. Sales people continue to sell the old products because that is easier.

Financial rewards signal what senior leadership thinks is most important, so it is a subtle but powerful tool. Aligning incentives just means paying for what you actually want people to do. Many compensation plans pay for one thing while management expects another.

That seems like the opposite of what you want to do.

It is—no wonder people are so confused! Who's going to follow you into battle if you reward competing behaviors?

But check this out. If you do the incentives well, you can get really good results.

Maynard Webb took advantage of this when he first joined eBay. As he began to gain control over the environment, Maynard wrote goals for himself and for everybody on his team, and made sure his counterparts in the business gave input. "We would all make quarterly commitments and then work those," he said.

Maynard went to an even higher level of shared goal-setting, though, and brought suppliers into the fold. "I would do these executive meet-and-greets with suppliers, and I would say, 'Hey, nice to meet you. Can I have your home phone and cell numbers?' They were like, 'Really?' and I would say, 'Yeah, really. I don't want to mess around with trying to get through to you. When we are down, we care about fixing it fast. In fact, I want you to link your bonus to eBay's up-time!'"

Amazingly, Maynard negotiated to do just that. "You can imagine how focused our suppliers were in helping us achieve our metrics. Our metrics were their bonus metrics!"

It sounds like helping my team maintain commitments involves constant vigilance. I need to communicate often, and recognize and reward my team regularly.

There are many other ways you could go about it, but those are definitely a few places to start.

In the end, the best way to maintain commitments is by ensuring your team always feels challenged. Fortunately, you have an opportunity every day as a leader to motivate your team to become their best selves.

CHALLENGED

"Best selves." I like that phrase.

It is a powerful idea. The greatest leaders in the world have a vision for their teams that often surpasses what they, themselves, think they can do.

Most of us are capable of achieving extraordinary things, but we limit ourselves out of fear or insecurity. Pass that fear or insecurity on to your team, and you'll end up with a whole group of fearful, insecure people who don't think they can do more than they are already doing.

Your job as a leader is to challenge each person on your team to become his or her best self, and to challenge the team itself to become its absolute best.

Is challenging people just another way of motivating them?

Absolutely, but it goes beyond the traditional definition of motivation where you do something *to* people. Most people's drive to succeed comes from within, so your job is to *bring out* the best in them.

What does that look like?

When that sales manager rightly critiqued Randy's weak leadership back at his former company, it completely fired him up to change. His team deserved better, and he knew he could be better for them.

An experience from many years earlier jumped to his mind. Randy does a lot of mountain climbing, and during one backpacking trip, one of his companions sprained his ankle so badly on a loose boulder that the group had to send an emergency party out of the mountains to get help. Randy was among the handful of climbers picked to go.

The group hiked down the mountain at a blistering, double-time pace—exhausting, grinding work that burned up much of the day. After calling for help, two of the members stayed behind while Randy and the leader of the group, Will, hiked back up to coordinate the rescue mission. It started raining during the climb, and dusk soon gave way to darkness while they were still miles away from the campsite. There was nothing fun about it. Will pushed Randy hard. He challenged him to be his very best. Amazingly, they climbed back to their companions in less time than they had spent coming down the mountain.

Was this at high altitude?

It was, which only made it harder. Randy learned an incredible lesson that day, though. He found he was capable of doing something far greater than he knew he could do. Will's unwavering belief in Randy was greater than Randy's own belief in himself.

That story came to mind when his sales team faltered all those years ago. He got in the field with them and challenged them with a vision bigger than they thought they could achieve. They had been selling five- and six-figure deals to local governments. He told them he believed they could sell multimillion-dollar deals to the state and federal government, and he would help them do it.

Most of the team refused to believe it, until one day, the

youngest and least experienced member of the sales force, Christie Acker, closed a seven-figure deal with the state of Mississippi.

That must have gotten people's attention!

It did. The more experienced salespeople suddenly believed and pushed hard to one-up Christie.

The impossible challenge became a rallying cry, and over the next few years, the team closed one deal after another, earning an award as the fastest-growing company in Atlanta at the time.

So part of a leader's job is pushing the team?

That's right, but not just because you're in a position to push. Pushing to tap into people's hidden reserves and awaken what is truly possible in them. Pushing to create commitment to do the seemingly impossible. Pushing to encourage, to inspire and motivate, not to intimidate. So many leaders get this wrong about getting relationships to work.

Pat Hughes inherited an underperforming region of a shingle manufacturer. It was so underperforming that at his first annual planning meeting, his new team was falling all over themselves to sign on to a piddling 3 percent year-over-year sales increase. Pat wasn't ready to raise a white flag, though. Instead, he called out "BS!" Then, when the shock had settled, he stood up, went to the whiteboard, and crossed out the 3 percent. In its place, he wrote 250 percent. As you can imagine, the team vehemently objected, but Pat challenged them anyway.

"BS"? That's intimidation!

It looked that way at first, but Pat believed in his team and wanted to support them. He immediately followed the challenge by offering the tools that they needed. And it worked. Team members grew sales 300 percent that year, 100 times greater than they were ready to settle for before Pat awakened their own desire to succeed.

But does the leader always have to jump in like that? If the P and W are on target, won't high-performing teams set high bars on their own?

Definitely, although sometimes you have to prime the pump. That's what John Zillmer did at Aramark even though his plan was a little off-the-wall—a team-building event that led to wild success.

Oh no, you aren't going to tell me I have to climb ropes or go summit Mount Everest with my nine direct reports, are you?

Nope, we're not going to suggest that, and you're right, a lot of team building is hokum, unless it's clearly tied to purpose and priorities.

Hmmm . . . go on.

John knew he had a tough road ahead when he was promoted to executive vice president of the Business Dining Group, which ran corporate cafeterias and executive dining rooms for Aramark.

Competitive pressure had commoditized the business to the point where growth had stagnated, margins were on the decline, and even the board had lost any hope. Early on, chair-

man Joe Neubauer introduced his new EVP with these memo-
rably defeatist words: "You know we don't expect much out of
the business, but we expect John will be a good custodian
of it."

"I could feel my face get flushed," John told us. "There was
no freaking way I was going to be a custodian of that business."

**I can see how that might have stirred John's competitive
juices.**

You bet. John's two key lieutenants at Aramark, Ed Evans
and Jack Donovan, felt the same way he did: None of them
wanted to settle for being merely a custodian. So they con-
vened their leadership team at an off-site in Elkhart Lake, Wisconsin, home of one of the premier auto racetracks in the
United States, Road America.

The first afternoon of the retreat, John laid out the poor
historical results. He didn't get into future goals at all. He just
laid out the record, then asked everybody to report to the
lobby at eight the next morning in a T-shirt, gym shorts, and
tennis shoes.

Uh-oh—team gymnastics! My worst nightmare!

It was probably the worst nightmare of a lot of the regional
VPs, too, and John didn't tip his hand until they had boarded
a van. When he told them they were heading to a Skip Barber
race-driving experience, they became even more nervous.
None of them had driven a racecar before.

By the end of that second day, though, something magical
began to happen. This group of underperforming regional
vice presidents were high-fiving and slapping one another on

the back. People who had rarely spoken to one another before reveled in the collective experience. A disparate group of leaders began to see themselves as a team.

The following morning, John brought them back together and said, "Okay, now you have had a great racing experience together. You have seen that you can learn new things. We don't have to do things the same old way anymore. What do you want to achieve next year?"

Here comes the challenge.

That's right. After a day of discussion, the group decided it wanted to double new business sales from $30 million to $60 million. In fact, they pushed themselves even harder, and increased the goal to $100 million. This far exceeded what John had expected to hear.

John accepted their goal and gave them another challenge. "I know you loved this driving experience. If we achieve these goals, we will all come back to Road America next year, but we won't do a one-day driving experience. We'll do a three-day racing school!" Everybody went crazy with excitement. They thought it was a fantastic idea.

How did they do?

Amazingly well. For every quarter they made their numbers, John sent out a note along with a piece of racing gear— racing gloves the first quarter, shoes the second, a racing bag the third, and individualized racing suits the fourth.

When the team came back together at the end of the year for the three-day racing school, John presented each member with custom helmets that included specialized logos for the group. By the time they got on the track, they were fully equipped with an Aramark race uniform, shoes, gloves, and helmet.

"Every quarter ended up creating more excitement and anticipation," John told us. "Obviously, the challenge aligned the entire group around the goal, and we achieved our one-hundred-million-dollar new-sales target and dramatically improved operating profits. Most important, it created a team. People started liking each other and wanted to work together. They began exchanging ideas and people, and provided support to each other because they understood the value in sharing. They liked to win."

Ummmm . . .

Yes?

I admire what John did, but taking a curve at 150 mph on two wheels scares me as much as trudging up Everest or group-diving into the Mariana Trench. What are other ways to challenge people that are a little more amped back?

Encourage direct feedback and mutual accountability. That might be the most fundamental way to challenge people in the sense that it keeps everybody honest.

Confession: I have trouble holding people accountable. It's my least favorite part of the job.

You are in good company. Only 7 percent of leaders excel at it. But here's the deal. People want to do a good job for you and for their colleagues. You do them a disservice when you don't offer feedback to help them grow, and you do the whole team a disservice when you don't hold someone accountable for falling short on some goal.

You don't have to be ugly about it. In fact, we suggest you approach it in the spirit of being helpful. When somebody slips off track, ask what she needs and how you can help. Offer feedback and coaching to help her find a way through. And if she just can't get it done, take her off the assignment and redeploy someone else to cover it.

If you have done a great job of hiring A Players, you'll find that most of your team thrives on your feedback, offers it in return, and even holds one another mutually accountable. They challenge one another to be the best they can be.

And a challenged team will remain a committed one.

So far, you have told me about times when relationships worked. What does it look like when they don't?

In one large retailer, the Finance and Operations teams did not work well together.

"Operations was not listening to us," the CFO told us. "They were all surprised by what kept happening in the business."

As it turns out, the finance people and the operations people were rarely in the same room for operating reviews. Each group knew what was going on within its own silo, but there were no problem-solving discussions across the groups.

This was a breakdown in coordination, and the results were catastrophic.

The company went bankrupt. Twice. In five years.

That's really hard to do—to bankrupt a company twice. You just don't see that very often.

The first time, Finance annoyed Operations by giving them

overly detailed reports that they didn't understand. The business leaders did not realize they were running out of cash.

The second time, aggressive spending by Operations violated debt covenants and suddenly thrust the company into Chapter 11 again.

This team wasn't coordinated, lacked commitment, and didn't work together, much less challenge themselves to achieve excellence. The relationships did not work, and they paid for it handsomely.

So here's my takeaway: To achieve relationships that work, leaders have to make sure that the team is coordinated; each member feels committed to the mission, the leader, and the team; and everybody feels challenged to accomplish even more than they dream they can do.

That's it. And relationships that work produce powerful teams that generate extraordinary results. That's what being a full PWR leader truly means.

Ready to rate your R?

Bring it on!

RATE THE RELATIONSHIPS IN YOUR ORGANIZATION

"I think our R = _____ on a scale of 1 (low) to 10 (high)."

SCALE	DESCRIPTION	CHECK THE BOX THAT DESCRIBES YOUR RELATIONSHIPS
1	"This place is like *Lord of the Flies*—total uncoordinated chaos. We have no hope of achieving good results."	☐
2	"Fire drills are the norm" or "We are reactive and not proactive—we don't review our performance or solve problems together." Or "Problems fester." "We are uncoordinated."	☐
3	"The left hand does not know what the right hand is doing" or "This place is highly political" or "We waste so much time and energy."	☐
4	"There is little coordination here" or "There is little accountability" or "We don't measure our goals versus actual results" or "Senior leadership says one thing but does another."	☐
5	"Some key relationships are not working well" or "People avoid confrontation" or "We are often out of sync and it impacts our results" or "Nobody challenges us."	☐
6	"We meet, but our meetings are not always a good use of time." Or "We suffer from having silos that don't talk to one another" or "Not everybody is committed."	☐
7	"Our relationships are pretty good" or "We meet and review performance regularly" or "We are mostly coordinated."	☐

8	"The relationships here are good and functional, but could be improved" or "This is mostly a meritocracy."	☐
9	"Nearly every relationship is working very well" or "We have a cadence of communication to make sure we are hitting our goals" or "We solve problems efficiently and effectively" or "We are universally committed to our mission."	☐
10	"The relationships here work like clockwork—internally, and with our external customers and partners," or "Senior leadership walks the talk," or "A real meritocracy," or "The right people are talking at the right time," or "Our meetings are highly productive and not at waste of time," or "We are achieving our goals because our people are incredibly committed" or "We are a well-oiled machine."	☐

5
EQUALS

The triathlon's over! I've got a score for all three stages. What next?

Multiply the P, W, and R values together to find your total PWR Score.

Done!

Then ask yourself, "How do we improve it?"

Your PWR Score helps you understand what you need to do. It's like your weight. If you don't like it, you exercise more or go on a diet, or maybe both.

In the case of your PWR Score, you want to improve your number to 729 or better.

Why 729 again?

Because 729 means you have rated each of your P, W, and R a 9. That is where you want to be, and it means that things are going well in every dimension.

And 1,000?

As we said earlier, it's not a useful goal. In fact we've never met a leader who has achieved it. But we have met many who operate at 729 or even a notch higher. Those are the top 1 percent leaders who truly shine.

I suppose it would help if I involved my team in calculating my PWR Score. How do I have a PWR Conversation to do that?

We recently had a PWR Conversation with an amazing leader, Reggie Bicha, and his team. He runs human services for the state of Colorado, a 5,000-person organization with a $2.5 billion budget. He and his team have won awards for being one of the very best in his field at improving metrics around caring for society's most vulnerable—children of abuse, the elderly in poverty, veterans, and people with mental health issues.

Not too long ago, Reggie had heard about *Power Score* and asked us to facilitate a PWR Conversation with his team. We were happy to volunteer some time in support of his worthy mission.

The outside of his building is misleadingly "government" looking. Picture a 1970s-era building, gray and dated, in some need of a fresh coat of paint. The inside of the room where we met looked a lot like an elementary school classroom, complete with one of those large round clocks on the wall.

Doughnuts, cookies, and carrots were in plastic trays on a table to the left as we entered the room. Reggie's team had arrived ten minutes early—they seemed like the social services, do-gooding types that you'd expect, but they had an air of urgency. Then Reggie arrived on the scene five minutes before the top of the hour.

Reggie, a six-foot-tall African American man, briskly walked through the doorway. His neatly trimmed goatee framed a warm smile when he saw his team. But his eyes burned with the intensity of a man on a mission.

Reggie knows hardship. He grew up in a neighborhood alongside many people struggling with poverty, disabilities, and abuse. He believed that his neighbors needed a hand up to a better life. And they needed that hand now. So when he was in college and graduate school, Reggie committed himself to a career in social service, and he did it with the empathy of knowing, exactly, what his "customer base" was living through.

One of his very first clients right out of school was a little girl. She was the youngest child in a family of six children. Her parents were alcoholics, were violent toward each other, and saw no future for themselves. As a child protection worker, Reggie had to place her into foster care for her own protection. But when he saw the pain in the girl's eyes as she looked at her mother, tears rolling down her face, he knew there had to be a better way.

"When I remember the look on that little girl's face," Reggie said, "I remember that it shouldn't have to be like this. I was put on this earth to make a difference for people like that girl and her family."

For Reggie, the success or failure of his team means life or death.

How did the conversation play out?

It went like this. Katherine Desmond, one of our colleagues, was the lead facilitator. She started by asking Reggie's team to think about this question:

"Are we running at full power?"

Katherine added, "What does it look like, or feel like, when a team runs at full power?"

Reggie let his team speak. They said things like "Running at full power is when the mission is clear and everybody knows what is expected of them." "Full power to me is when you look at your colleagues and there are no bad apples on the team, and you are proud to be a part of a special group who respects each other." "You feel like everyone is rowing in the same direction. You are not wasting your time. It's efficient." "Everything hums."

A man in a navy sport coat piped up: "I think of full power as more than just meeting the bare minimum. It is when the team crushes the goals." Reggie added, "Yes, and full power to me means we are doing our best. In our case, it means delivering the best possible results for the children and families in our state."

Katherine asked, "What's your Power Score?" Not knowing quite what she meant, the team looked at one another with uncertainty.

"Let's calculate this team's Power Score," Katherine continued. "Everybody, please take out a piece of paper and a pen. Please write down these three letters in big letters: P, W, and R.

- P stands for priorities—Do we have the right *priorities*?
- W stands for who—Do we have the right *who*?
- R stands for relationships—Do we have the right *relationships*?

Katherine added, "Please rate each letter, P, W, and R on a one-to-ten scale. One is low and ten is high. That's right, take a couple of minutes and work on your own."

Once they had all put their pens down, Katherine said, "Almost there. Now multiply the three numbers together and write down the answer. That is this team's Power Score."

Eyebrows went up.

The energy in the room changed, as if there were a sudden drop in barometric pressure.

Chairs squeaked in the silence as people shifted. Some laughed nervously.

"Everybody, hold up your scores. Just like the Olympics, or *Dancing with the Stars*. And with a total possible of one thousand, this team's scores are! . . ."

280
343
448
180
512
360
315

And two team members both put up a PWR Score of 432 and snickered.

Everyone nervously looked at Reggie.

Reggie let out a wistful whistle. "Wow. Although this team wins awards and we feel great about our work, it's clear that we don't think we are running anywhere near our full potential."

He was clearly disappointed that the PWR Score was not

higher, but he did not take offense at the low scores. He later told us, "I took it as my team caring about the work we do. And wanting to make our impact stronger."

Reggie turned to the two people who scored the team a 432. "You both gave us a score of 432. What were your P, W, and R scores?"

The first person said, "I went with an 8 for priorities. I think we have done a good job connecting our mission to actual goals and expectations, right?" Everyone around the circle nodded. "But I gave our W only a 6 for our organization. And that was more around feeling that we really have struggled with hiring and having the right people at the frontline supervisor level and this has hurt us. And I gave our relationships a 9—I think everyone in this organization is committed to what we are doing. Plus, we all get along well, communicate well, and we have our eyes on the critical metrics so there is no mystery how we are performing."

The second person with a 432 said, "I gave exactly the same scores: 8 for P, 6 for W, and 9 for R. But what came up for me is thinking that we probably have too many priorities. We waste time on things that don't matter as much. That's why I marked us down to an 8 for P, priorities. On the W, the who, I agree that we seem to get hiring right at the senior levels and with our caregivers on the front line, but our supervisor hiring is really not as reliable for some reason. So I guess I agree that W is our weakest area, and specifically at that on-site supervisor and manager level. R seems good. The meetings and the constant follow-up on all our metrics work well. Maybe we could push ourselves to get past the thirty-thousand-foot level, where we spend so much time, and focus more on how things are going at the thousand-foot level with specific site locations."

After about forty minutes of further discussion about why people chose the scores they did and what they could do to improve them, Katherine moved to wrap up.

She said, "Three things are clear: One: This team really wants to increase its Power Score." There were nods around the table and plenty of yeses. "Two: You all are pretty consistent in your ratings of your current score." More nods. "And three: You have really cut to the chase and revealed the specific issues that hold you back from running at full power along the P, the W, and the R." The group agreed once again.

So how did it end with Reggie and his team?

At forty-five minutes after the hour, Reggie turned to his key lieutenant, Nikki. "So what are our next steps?"

Nikki flipped up her pad of paper and said, "Three things. First, it sounds like we are going to make frontline supervisor hiring and management a top priority. Second, it sounds like we need Susan and Dee to get together to come up with a plan for improving communications about our priorities, and cascading it down to individual expectations. Third, I'd say let's have this Power Conversation on a regular basis, just to check ourselves and track our progress. Melissa, can you add our Power Score to the list of metrics that we monitor and discuss every Senior Leadership Team monthly meeting?"

The team agreed and Reggie adjourned the meeting. He paused as he walked out.

Turning toward us, he said, "Thank you. This Power Conversation was so clarifying. I did not want to say this publicly, but we had a two-day-long strategic off-site two months ago. And I have to tell you"—Reggie pointed to the large round clock on the wall—"we accomplished more in the past fifty-five minutes with this approach than we accomplished in two full days of strategic planning."

Maybe he was just being nice.

Yes, maybe.

But we are confident that having your own PWR Conversation will be the most useful hour your team has ever spent together.

Okay, point me in the right direction.

Here's a simple script to make it very easy the first time you do it.

1. **Are we running at full power?** (5 minutes) Ask your team to describe what it feels like to run at full power and what it feels like to fall short. They will tell you about times in their careers when things just clicked and times when things felt clunky and hard.
2. **Do we have the right priorities?** (2 minutes) Without revealing their answers, ask them to rate the team's priorities on a 1-to-10 scale, reminding them that a perfect 10 requires that the priorities are:
    a. *Connected to the mission* in a compelling way.
    b. *Correct* and likely to produce the right results.
    c. *Clear* so that everybody understands the critical few.
3. **Do we have the right who?** (2 minutes) Ask them to

rate the strength of the people on your team on a 1-to-10 scale, where higher scores go to the teams with the most A Players—people who can achieve the priorities in the right ways. Ask them to think about where the team has been properly:

    a. *Diagnosed* with a clear plan to address gaps.

    b. *Deployed* with the right people in the right jobs and a hiring process in place to select A Players to the team.

    c. *Developed* to ensure the team can play to their strengths while building new skills for the future.

4. **Do we have the right relationships?** (2 minutes) Ask them to rate how well the relationships work on a 1-to-10 scale, where the highest scores go to those rare and powerful teams that produce exceptional results. Ask them to think about whether the people on your team are:

    a. *Coordinated.* The right people talk to one another at the right times, share key information, and review metrics.

    b. *Committed.* The team buys into the mission, trusts you as a leader, and supports one another on the journey.

    c. *Challenged.* Each member of the team is highly motivated and pushes the others to be their best selves. The team gives one another feedback and practices mutual accountability.

5. **Now multiply your P, W, and R scores together and write the number boldly on a sheet of paper** (1 min-

ute). Remind them that the resultant PWR Score should be a number between 1 and 1,000. They may use a calculator if they need it!

6. **On the count of three, let's all hold up our PWR Scores.** (3 minutes) After the numbers are all visible, give everyone a minute to look at one another's scores. Often, they'll see a startling range, which is perfectly fine. Next, ask one member of your team to write the PWR Scores on the board. If you want, have them capture the individual P, W, and R scores as well.

7. **We have a nice range of PWR Scores. Let's look at why we each came out where we did.** (30 minutes) Now facilitate a conversation to explore various numbers. Start with some of the higher scores. Why did they rate as highly as they did? Now work your way down to some of the lower scores. What opportunities for improvement do they see?

8. **Let's discuss next steps.** (10 minutes) Decide how you are going to prioritize what you heard in the PWR Conversation, to whom you are going to assign key tasks, and how you will follow up and measure results.

9. **We will have another PWR Conversation in ninety days.** You can choose a shorter interval, such as monthly if you are moving very quickly, but quarterly works for most teams.

10. **Thank you.** Thank your team for participating and for helping you lead the team at full power.

Helpful. So I know what I am shooting for, what does running at full PWR look like?

Jim Goodnight at SAS. As far as we can tell, Jim has operated at full PWR throughout most of SAS's history. We had the opportunity to visit the SAS Institute campus in Cary, North Carolina. It looked like utopia.

Come on. Utopia?

Yup, utopia. Like "rolling hills dotted with solar panels and fluffy sheep cheerfully eating the grass around the solar panels, which provide clean energy to the company" utopia.

Like "parents gathered around tables in the cafeteria feasting on organic kale salad that was grown on the property, next to their smiling kids who attend school right there on campus" utopia!

Like "Tony Stark's high-tech and gorgeous *Iron Man 3* headquarters shots were taken right there at SAS headquarters" utopia!

I can't believe I've never heard of this company.

You're not alone. For years now, SAS been named one of *Fortune*'s "Best Companies to Work For," but because the company is privately held, you don't see them in the news as much as Apple or Google.

The company makes money, too. SAS has remained profitable and has grown *every year* since Jim founded it in 1976. Revenue has grown from $138,000 that first year to over $3 billion today, making it the largest independent software company in the world.

Okay, okay, so I'm very impressed. How did they do that? What's Jim's secret? He must be the most charismatic leader in the world.

No, he is quite soft-spoken, actually. But he has a knack for the P, the W, and the R. He is a triple threat.

First, we would rate his P a 10. He has been singularly focused on innovating one core product set for nearly forty years. In fact, his only priority is for SAS to be at the leading edge of innovation in data and analytics. Period. So he made the decision to invest an incredible 25 percent of revenue into R&D every year. He interacts with customers often, both individually and at SAS Global Forum, a customer-managed conference that is also the largest annual gathering of SAS users. He encourages customers to suggest ideas for future software releases online via the SASware Ballot. SAS prioritizes and delivers requests.

We rate his W a 9.5. As we shared earlier, he hires incredibly smart people and then gives them a lot of room to learn and grow. When leaders struggle on an assignment, he reassigns them so they can perform as an A Player somewhere else. His team is among the most talented we have seen, and they are proud to be there.

We rate his R a 9.5 as well. Jim has created reporting cadences that make sense—constantly reviewing strategy and goals. He does videoconferences for the whole company to communicate priorities and progress. He has regularly scheduled "Java with Jim" small coffee meetings with employees. Not only that, but have you heard of "managing by walking around"? Well, Jim *lives* on his company's campus. He's always around. And he has created an environment of openness, collaboration, and mutual accountability, so employees actually tell him what they think. The relationships really work at SAS, his team is incredibly loyal, and the results prove it.

SAS's PWR Score is $P \times W \times R = 10 \times 9.5 \times 9.5 = 903$ out of 1,000. SAS is definitely running at full power.

At age seventy-two, Jim Goodnight has no interest in slowing down. He does not seem stressed, despite the complexity and scale of the enterprise he and his team have built. He said, "Oh, I love this job so much. The customers. The products. The people. I love it all."

I would love to love my job that way.

Totally. And you can. Life is short.

We see people who run at full power loving their jobs a lot more than people whose teams are not yet running at full power.

You can, too.

What's another story of running at full power? Is it possible for lightning to strike twice in the same industry?

Yes. Intuit is another software company that runs at full power. And we feel personal appreciation for Scott Cook and Intuit's products.

Intuit makes Quicken, which we use to manage our personal family finances. We have almost never had an argument about money with our spouses, thanks to Scott Cook, founder of Intuit! We set financial goals, track our spending, and stay on budget. Easy.

Intuit also makes QuickBooks, the financial software we have used from day one at ghSMART. Geoff remembers when he printed the firm's first invoice on Quicken. It was like magic. You do work for a client. You enter it into QuickBooks, print it out, and send it. And the client, if they are happy with the value of the work, pays you. Geoff was so enamored with this technology that he used to jot personal notes of thanks to clients at the top of the QuickBooks invoices.

When we started our research, we contacted Scott Cook and told him we are big fans of his work, and that we would love to hear his story and see if it fit the theme of this book.

And you got time with him?

Sure did. Scott was great, and he also suggested that we interview his current CEO, Brad Smith, who is also a super-impressive leader.

Scott founded Intuit in 1983. He had previously worked at Procter & Gamble, then at Bain & Company consulting. He was inspired by the goal of helping people manage their finances, and he wanted the product to be intuitive and easy to use. Thus—Intuit.

He told us, "The purpose of business is to make people's lives better."

That is fantastic. I love that attitude. He sounds like a great leader.

He is. He is really nice and very humble, too. His CEO, Brad, told us, "When Scott Cook introduces himself, he tells you that he works for a software company in Mountain View. What he doesn't say up front is that he founded Intuit!"

So what are Intuit's secrets?

This is a story of always keeping an eye on the customer and building an organization that aspires to do a small number of things very well.

We would rate Intuit's priorities, P, a 9.

Just as Intuit was starting to really take off, Scott decided it was time to write down the company's mission and values— the "why" that would help shape the "what" of its priorities.

"When we were smaller," Scott told us, "everyone had a chance to work with me and knew what was important to me. When we got to five hundred people, that was no longer possible. Plus we were growing fast, which made it harder to encode the values in our team."

Today, Intuit is guided by eight core values: (1) Integrity Without Compromise, (2) We Care and Give Back, (3) Be Bold, (4) Be Passionate, (5) Be Decisive, (6) Learn Fast, (7) Win Together, and (8) Deliver Awesome.

Not only that, but Intuit has also been very good at articulating the "what" of its priorities. This includes having the courage to change priorities as markets shifted. CEO Brad Smith recalled one of those times. "Mobile technology was becoming a big deal. I remember this one day we had a company-wide broadcast, and we said that we feel like *football* champions now standing in the middle of a *baseball* diamond."

What did he mean by that?

The market had changed. They were masters of building software for desktops, but now everything was going mobile. "We had the wrong uniform on," Brad said. "We didn't understand the rules of the new game. We were about to step into the next chapter of our growth and we had to figure it out. It became known as our connected service strategy."

That sounds like a critical time for Intuit.

It was. They realized their priorities were incorrect, so rather than continuing down that path, they reset them. They came up with new priorities that were correct, clear, and connected to their mission.

Did that impact the team?

Absolutely! New priorities forced Scott and Brad to reexamine the players they had on the field. Brad said, "We ended up moving 71 percent of our leaders around to get the right people in the right roles to execute our new strategy." That is a lot of change, but they courageously got it done.

Intuit's W could have been much lower, but thanks to their attention to making changes when the strategy changed, they ended up with the right people in the right seats. We rate Intuit's who, W, a 9.

So what about relationships? Do they get results?

You bet.

Intuit has reporting cadences that fit the urgency of whether an outcome is short-term, medium-term, or longer-term priority.

Intuit follows an innovation methodology pioneered by Geoffrey Moore called horizon planning. As Brad explained, "Every leader has to keep his current business on track but also place bets for the next chapter and the chapter further out. We invest 60 percent, 30 percent, and 10 percent of our resources into these three horizons.

"As it turns out, people who want to focus on the first horizon are like an Ivy League rowing crew. They love being in this systemic sort of organization and pulling as one. Those in the second horizon are the sort of people who love white-water rafting—adrenaline junkies who are in it for the thrill of the ride. They hit rocks and fall out of the boat, but they just grab each other and push on. Those in the third horizon are intellectually curious, discovery-driven people searching for sunken treasure. They dive down ten times and come up empty nine of those times, but once in a while they will come up with gold that is just phenomenal. In all three cases, we match people to their passions."

That's it? The big secret?

They track metrics, too. Scott is a big fan of business plans with clear goals and metrics. He said, "Every management meeting starts with key metrics. What are the metrics that matter, and how are we doing on them?"

On top of that, the leaders of Intuit are great role models. Brad said, "We are humble because Scott modeled humility. We are generous and self-effacing because Bill Campbell, our chairman and former CEO, was generous and self-effacing. We are rigorous and attentive to execution because my predecessor, Steve Bennett, modeled execution. I have learned from each of them and try to model the culture they helped create."

Lastly, they constantly encourage and challenge their team. Brad said, "Our job as leaders is not to put the greatness into people but to recognize the greatness that already exists and to create the environment that brings it out. That philosophy guides us at Intuit."

We rate Intuit's relationships, R, a 10.

Intuit's PWR Score is $P \times W \times R = 9 \times 9 \times 10 = 810$ out of 1,000. Right?

Right. Intuit is definitely running at full power.

And it is working. The company has grown from $3 billion to over $4 billion under Brad's leadership while more than doubling its market capitalization.

Okay, the superstars are "super"—by definition, I guess. But you said yourself that most leaders are nowhere near full power. What does it normally look like?

Most leaders fall short of running their teams at full power when they first start out, but that's okay. Use the PWR Conversation to calculate your PWR Score, and then figure out what you need to do to improve your score.

Kinko's offers an example of a big company that stumbled and then regained its footing. They had a clash that nearly killed the company. Watch what happened to the business as its leaders improved its PWR Score.

The company had been founded in 1970 by Paul Orfalea with a single copy machine strategically placed on a sidewalk near the University of California, Santa Barbara. Orfalea grew the business using an unusual legal structure. Rather than setting up corporate stores or franchising the operation, Paul had created personal partnerships with each of the 127 store managers.* Consequently, each Kinko's ran fairly independently. Store managers made their own decisions about what products to sell, how to sell them, how to price, and how to manage customer service. That was a source of strength in the early years but turned into an open wound once Kinko's had hundreds of stores.

Private equity firm Clayton, Dubilier & Rice (CDR) purchased about a third of the business on the theory that Kinko's would be more successful if each store operated as part of a unified whole rather than as an independent federation of independent stores. The founder, Paul, stayed on as chairman of the board.

Uh-oh, I can see the problem coming.

You got it. Orfalea the founder wanted to stick to the priority of letting the store managers do their own thing. But the owners wanted the whole network to have more of a centralized set of priorities they controlled.

So the P was mutually exclusive. You can't do both.

We talked with Kinko's former head of HR Paul Rostron, who witnessed this conflict firsthand. "We spent the better part of the first eighteen or twenty-four months I was there fighting about this," he told us. "The P score was at best a 2 out of 10."

To make matters worse, fiefdoms of the "old guard" still

* Paul Orfalea and Ann Marsh, *Copy This! How I Turned Dyslexia, ADHD, and 100 Square Feet into a Company Called Kinko's* (New York: Workman, 2007).

wanted autonomy for the stores, which was in direct conflict with what CDR wanted. No wonder, the W score was around a 5 out of 10. The holdouts might have been talented, but they definitely were not on board.

You can imagine how the lack of clarity about priorities, hodgepodge of misaligned managers, and daily turmoil made the relationships ineffective. The score there was a dismal 2 out of 10.

So the company's PWR Score was hovering around a $2 \times 5 \times 2 = 20$ out of 1,000.

That is terrible. But Kinko's didn't fail. How did it pull through?

First, by addressing the P, the priorities, and almost simultaneously, by dealing with the W, the who.

Let me guess—the folks from CDR finally put their foot down.

They did. They installed one of their operating partners as an interim CEO to figure out what was going on and quickly realized they had to put an end to the competing priorities.

They bought out the founder and removed him from the company. Then they hired a new CEO and moved the business from Southern California to Dallas. "We did that so we could completely rebuild the management team," Paul said. "Finally, we pursued a new business model that supported the vision of maximizing the value of the network verses running Kinko's on a store-by-store basis. It created instant alignment of priorities."

With agreement about the strategy, and clear metrics put in

place to drive it, the P climbed to a 9. "This became the inflection point that turned the company around," Paul explained.

How did they improve their W score from there?

The new CEO and management team started hiring leaders who fit the strategy throughout the network of what became 1,200 stores. Paul said, "We did a bunch of analysis around our top managers and learned that those with the best leadership DNA outperformed those with the most intellectual horse-power by a factor of two-to-one. Those with both leadership DNA and intellectual horsepower were four times stronger than average. We staffed our hubs with those as much as possible." W organization-wide climbed to an 8 out of 10 and rising.

Did relationships work?

They began to. The basic coordination and operating cadence of meetings, metrics, dashboards, and follow-up allowed the senior leaders right down to the first-line supervisors to know how their performance stacked up relative to expectations. "It all came down to being clear about our objectives," Paul said. "Once we had alignment there, we could hire the right leadership team and focus them on the right priorities. As we got traction with our results, it created even more alignment on our direction and commitment to pursuing it. It became a self-reinforcing system."

R climbed to at least a 7 out of 10, although it took some time to break old habits.

So Kinko's PWR Score climbed from a low of 20 to 504 ($9 \times 8 \times 7$), which is the level where teams start humming.

And the results? How did they do financially?

Profit was at $100 million and declining when Paul Rostron started his job and all of the turmoil was happening. After the changes, profits doubled to $200 million, same-store sales tripled their growth rates, employee satisfaction improved significantly, customer satisfaction metrics went up, and the investors earned an attractive 3.5-times return on their investment. It was a home run for everyone.

What about more of an entrepreneurial example. That is risky business.

Jeff Booth is a great example of someone who went from low PWR to full PWR over time, and his success rose right alongside the improvement to his score.

Jeff is an entrepreneur in Canada who was running a building company. The inefficiency in that industry was driving him nuts. In one case, while building a customer's home, flooring materials that Jeff's company provided didn't arrive on time. He had to force the family to put all of their furniture in storage and move to a cramped hotel on the other side of town. The man's wife and children were not happy.

Ouch!

Ouch is right. "You could get lucky as a builder or you could hope that your suppliers were trustworthy," Jeff said. "Mostly, you just got screwed over because they had all the knowledge. You took delays and paid higher prices than you should all the time.

"Using the PWR framework, I'd say we had a very low Power Score at that time," Jeff told us. "We were just wholesaling building supplies the old-fashioned way—using the phone, working through distributors. It was all so inefficient.

"Our P based on that business model was a 3 out of 10. And I had employed some of my friends from growing up, and while their hearts were in the right place, they were unable to resolve any of the problems that came up in the supply chain. My W was a 4 out of 10. They worked in fits and starts, too. I don't think they ever knew their goals and didn't communicate very well. That was my fault as much as theirs. We were half as effective as we should have been. It was incredibly inefficient. I would give our R a 5 out of 10.

"So $3 \times 4 \times 5 = 60$. Our PWR Score was only 60 out of 1,000! We had bland priorities, the wrong who, and nothing special about the relationships we had inside or outside our company. In hindsight, it was no wonder we weren't making any money."

That's pretty bad!

Hard to score much lower, but Jeff didn't take it lying down.

The relative lack of success triggered a new career goal. Jeff decided he wanted to revolutionize the building supply industry—to help the end customers and their builders get great prices on high-quality materials and receive them on time on budget.

"My co-founder and friend, Robert Banks, and I had a big vision for how we could tackle this five-hundred-billion-dollar market. It started out as just the two of us, and we thought we could do it all. As it turns out, the vision was right, but the way we tackled it was wrong."

What happened?

Jeff and Robert started with the P. "We set out to change the industry," Jeff said. "We wanted to create a new channel that would reduce the chaos and the friction."

Jeff realized he could forge relationships with key suppliers and offer materials directly to the buyer over the Internet, cutting out all of the middlemen that had given him so many sleepless nights over missed delivery dates. This virtually guaranteed a radical reduction in missed shipments and delays.

He rewrote his entire business plan and renamed his company BuildDirect. He focused exclusively on flooring materials so he could build relationships directly with the manufacturers.

"My P rose over time from a 3 to a 9. Every year, we narrowed and narrowed and narrowed so that our priorities became tighter and tighter."

How did these new priorities fit with his old team?

They didn't. Serendipitously, a friend had recommended that he read our book *Who* right around this time. "It was like a lightbulb went on," Jeff said. "I realized that I needed different people. I needed people around me who shared a sense of purpose to revolutionize the industry. And the skill set I needed was totally different from what I had. My new plan was all execution risk, and execution risk is basically all people risk."

What did he do?

He built scorecards for the whole company and then started

hiring a completely different type of person. "That is when I stopped hiring traditional industry people and instead hired mathematicians and programmers," he said. "We were not going to make the industry more efficient by doing it the same way it had been done for four thousand years. We needed more of an Internet-savvy skill set to operate almost like a trading floor—finding deals and using large quantities of data to find the right materials at the right price that we could get to the builders on time and on budget. We ended up exiting many of the building industry people on the team. It was a radical departure."

A building supply company hiring programmers and mathematicians? That's strange.

It may be strange, but it made sense given the priorities that Jeff wanted to achieve. He wanted to automate the industry for buying and selling building supplies and cut costs by cutting out the middleman.

The new math geniuses who joined BuildDirect conducted advanced analytics and created specialized algorithms that enabled the company to take control of the market rather than remain victims of it. They found ways to coordinate container ships to ensure that certain products at certain prices went to certain places. They shared data back to their manufacturers so they could produce more of the right products at the right times. They literally made markets. All of this created vastly more value for customers.

Jeff said, "My W score went from 4 to 9 over the next couple of years."

So after he hired the new who, what did he do next?

He turned attention to the R, the relationships. His team established key relationships with external partners, to feed them the data they needed to make the market more efficient.

The biggest problem was internally, though. Even though he had gotten the P and W right, relationships weren't working as well as he wanted. That got him thinking. "There is a question in *Who* that I find incredibly powerful: 'How will your boss rate you on a 1-to-10 scale?' We found that you could take people whose bosses would rate them a 10 and drop them on the moon, and they will create a civilization for you. The 4s, 5s, and 6s would always blame somebody else for their problems. The amazing thing is that they didn't realize that the problem was actually them.

"That got me thinking. Can I say I am a 10 in all aspects of my life? The truth was, I could for my relationships, but not for my business. It was still running in fits and starts. I could either say it was everybody else and the world is doing it to me, or I could say it was something I was doing to create this. That epiphany—that it was something I was doing—helped me realize I still wasn't enabling and developing my team to be as successful as I needed it to be."

That's incredibly insightful, but what did he do?

He set up a huddle process to discuss progress. "We celebrate good news, review status on the outcomes and KPIs that support those outcomes, dig into where people are stuck, and check in on how they are feeling.

"What I have found from our huddle process is that if you

want to create a learning organization, you have to spend time talking about where people are stuck and help them get unstuck. The natural tendency for a leader is to punish them for not knowing what to do. If you do that, you'll never hear them talking about where they are stuck in a huddle again. You have to celebrate those mistakes and those 'stucks' and learn from them. You have to have in-depth discussions about them so you can help each other get unstuck. You have to make it safe to have a great debate, free of politics. In our model, if you are not stuck on a regular basis, you are not pressing hard enough."

I can see how Jeff both coordinated and challenged his team in his huddle. Did it improve his R?

It did. And here's the really neat thing. Remember how he wrote scorecards earlier? Well, he gave them to his team, and they took them really seriously. Jeff said, "In most companies, you see people sandbagging their goals during the budgeting process. Here we have a team of A Players who want to win, so we see them pushing their targets even higher. I have to ask them what they will take off their scorecard to enable them to achieve it. Outcomes keep getting more aggressive, not less aggressive.

"We have great leaders who want to challenge and debate the process. It has created great alignment and great performance. My R went from five to nine."

We believe it, too. While Jeff's PWR Score climbed from 60 to 729, his revenue climbed from $20 million, where he had plateaued for over a decade, to $150 million in just four years. And the company is still growing rapidly.

Even more important, customers no longer spend the night in cramped hotels on account of delays. Instead, they sleep in their own beds in their dream homes, right on schedule.

What does it feel like to be part of a winning team like that, I wonder?

Very good, if Jeff is any guide. We recently visited him at his bustling new offices in Vancouver. Jeff greeted us on the ground floor lobby and told us, "The company's growth has been like a rocket ship. It has been the most amazing experience for all of us." Then he gave us the tour.

BuildDirect was taking over two new floors and the entire adjoining building. As Jeff glided around his office, people looked up from their computer screens, stood up and smiled, and high-fived Jeff. You could see how proud he was of this successful team, and how proud they were to be part of it. They all know they are making a positive impact on the world, and that is the best kind of success.

YOUR TURN

We hope the PWR Conversation becomes the most useful hour you have ever spent with your team. And we *know* the PWR Score will give you deep insight into what you need to do to improve your leadership and increase your chances of success. Ultimately, we want you to operate at full power with a full-powered team.

As you've seen, many of the leaders profiled in this book

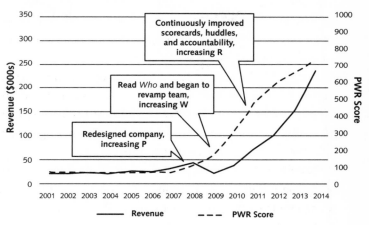

Power Score and Revenue for Jeff Booth (2001–2014)

Source: Jeff Booth

began with low PWR Scores but took action to lead at full power. They set clear priorities, got the right who on their teams, and encouraged relationships to work.

Imagine how much better life will be when everybody runs their teams at full power.

Companies running at full power produce more valuable products and services for customers, offer more fulfilling employment opportunities for employees, create more wealth for owners, and produce more tax revenue to fund our governments.

Governments running at full power convert tax revenue into better services and outcomes that improve the quality of life in a society.

Hospitals operating at full power save more lives and care for us when we are sick.

Schools operating at full power prepare more children to become productive members of society and assume more leadership positions.

Leaders running at full power improve the standard of living for all of us.

Now it is your turn.

How do you want to impact the world? What difference do you want to make?

We don't want you to leave this conversation merely *feeling* differently about leading your team or just *thinking* new thoughts.

We want you out there, *doing* things differently!

We want you to run your team at full power and make your dreams come true.

We want you to experience what Jeff Booth and so many other leaders we profiled in this book are experiencing. "Our business is actually getting easier and easier," Jeff told us. "Most people would say that their business gets more chaotic as it grows. I think it is getting easier because I am around a team of A Players who want to win. I am having more fun. Plus, I have more time with my family and friends."

Life is better at full power, and it feels great.

You'll feel comfort in clarifying your priorities and knowing exactly why they matter and what you need to do to accomplish them. You will feel like you can count on your teammates more because the right *who* will be in the right *where* pursuing the right *what*. And the relationships are the best part—the camaraderie of being on a winning team is like nothing else in the world.

You now have the power to do that—to achieve whatever matters most to you and the people you serve. You have the power to pursue goals that you find meaningful and worthwhile. You have the power to make a difference that only you can make.

Archimedes, the classical Greek scientist and philosopher, once said, "Give me a place to stand, and a lever long enough, and I will move the world."

We believe leadership is the lever that has that power.

What do you say? Are you ready to run at full power, to move the world?

Acknowledgments

This book was really fun to write. We greatly appreciate those who made it possible.

- To our ghSMART clients who allow us the privilege to serve as their leadership advisors.
- To the 15,000+ leaders we have assessed, and the thousands we have advised.
- To the 55 leaders who shared their perspective and stories in original interviews we conducted just for this book: Christie Acker, Bill Amelio, Panos Anastassiadis, Claire Bennett, John Berisford, Reggie Bicha, Jeff Booth, Stephen Cerrone, Scott Clawson, Jim Clifton, Art Collins, Scott Cook, Mike D'Ambrose, Tom DiDonato, Jim Donald, Jeff Ewing, Michael Feinberg, Mike Feiner, Caperton Flood, Michael Fries, Atul Gawande, Bill George, Noel Ginsburg, Jim Goodnight, Robert Hanson, Verne Harnish, Larissa Herda, David Hoover, Pat Hughes, Aaron Kennedy, Wendy Kopp, David Levin, Tim Marquez, Mark Miller, Eva Moskowitz, Arthur

Peponis, Paul Rostron, Steven Rothstein, Joyce Russell, Kristin Russell, Mitchell Schear, Josh Silverman, Matt Simoncini, Brad Smith, Fred Smith, Juergen Stark, Brian Stolz, Razor Suleman, Michael Summers, Tim Tassopoulos, Kent Thiry, Pamela Thomas-Graham, Maynard Webb, Norman Weeks, John Zillmer.

- Thanks to our research teams at the University of Chicago, led by Steve Kaplan, and Columbia University, led by Morten Sorensen.
- To Leslie Rith-Najarian, a Ph.D. candidate in clinical psychology at the University of California, Los Angeles, and SPSS guru. She helped us with some of our statistical analyses.
- To Helen and Lorin Rees, our literary agents.
- To Ryan Doherty, Nina Shield, and Jennifer Tung, our editors at Ballantine/Random House.
- To Howard Means, who helped sharpen our writing.
- To the leaders who reviewed early drafts, including Reggie Bicha, Atul Gawande, Tyler Nottberg, and John Zillmer, each of whom provided particularly useful feedback.
- To Elena Botelho for securing and conducting several of the interviews.
- To Jim Intagliata and Eric Gerber, who pressure-tested our analysis.
- To our entire ghSMART team for contributing the data and ideas that produced the concept of PWR.

Further Reading

If you want more inspiration to achieve full power, we suggest the following:

Priorities

- Simon Sinek's book *Start with Why* will help you to clarify why your organization exists.
- Michael E. Porter's *Competitive Strategy* describes the five forces that act on every organization as it sets priorities—customers, existing competitors, new entrants, substitutes, and suppliers.
- Peter Drucker invented the term "management by objectives" (MBOs) and was a proponent of the idea that management is doing things right, and leadership is doing the right things. See *The Effective Executive,* an oldie but goodie—his shortest, and top-selling book.

- Eliyahu M. Goldratt's book *The Goal* is a business novel that teaches the reader about setting and achieving goals through removing constraints. Prioritization is at the root of identifying and removing constraints.
- *The 4 Disciplines of Execution: Achieving Your Wildly Important Goals* is one of the best books we have seen on priorities. McChesney, Covey, and Huling explain the important difference between setting goals around a small number of important "lag measures" that matter but that you don't directly control versus "leading measures" you can control, and the importance of having a visible dashboard that everyone can see.

Who

- *Who: The A Method for Hiring* by Geoff Smart and Randy Street. Learn more about the four steps to achieve a 90 percent hiring success rate: scorecard, source, select, and sell. And read the full story about how an interviewer got a candidate to admit that he slapped his CEO.
- *The One Thing You Need to Know* by Marcus Buckingham, to remind you to play to your strengths as a leader, and to hire people with strengths you lack.

Relationships

- *What Got You Here Won't Get You There,* by Marshall Goldsmith. Learn more about the twenty behavioral derailers that prevent leaders from building relationships that work.
- *The Leadership Challenge,* by Jim Kouzes and Barry Posner. Their Leadership Practices Inventory questionnaire has been given to 1.4 million leaders. The authors provide insights into building relationships that work. Their Five Practices of Exemplary Leadership: to model the way, inspire a shared vision, challenge the process, enable others to act, and encourage the heart.
- *The Checklist Manifesto,* by Atul Gawande, to convince yourself about the value of making a simple list of what matters, and reviewing it with the right people at the right times to achieve good outcomes.
- *The Five Dysfunctions of a Team,* by Pat Lencioni, to be on the lookout for when your team lacks trust, fears conflict, lacks commitment, avoids accountability, and does not attend to team results.
- *True North,* by Bill George and Peter Sims. Ideas and stories about how to "walk the talk" and show authenticity as a leader.
- Anything by Jim Collins (*Built to Last, Good to Great, Great by Choice*) or Verne Harnish (*The Rockefeller Habits*) is a useful reminder about the importance of discipline in setting goals and following up to achieve great results.

- *The Talent Code,* by Daniel Coyle, offers practical tips for how to be a great coach (e.g., constant nudges versus annual reviews).
- *Help Them Grow or Watch Them Go: Career Conversations Employees Want,* by Beverly Kaye and Julie Winkle Giulioni. This is a very useful book about how to have regular career conversations with employees.

About the Authors

GEOFF SMART, RANDY STREET, and ALAN FOSTER work at ghSMART, a consulting firm that helps leaders hire and develop talented teams and run them at full power. ghSMART was named one of the "world's top firms" in Broderick's *The Art of Managing Professional Services,* and was profiled in Atul Gawande's *The Checklist Manifesto,* Tom Peters's *The Little Big Things,* and George Anders's *The Rare Find.* The firm is the subject of two Harvard Business School cases, titled "ghSMART & Co.: Pioneering in Professional Services."

GEOFF SMART

Geoff serves as Chairman and Founder of ghSMART.

He is the co-author, with his colleague Randy Street, of the *New York Times* bestselling book *Who: The A Method for Hiring. Shanghai Daily* named *Who* a "Top 5 Business Book in China" and Canada's *Globe and Mail* named it the "#1 Best

Business and Management Book of 2009." Geoff is author of the number-one *Wall Street Journal* bestseller *Leadocracy: Hiring More Great Leaders (Like You) into Government,* which won the 2012 IPPY Gold Medal for Best Business Book of the Year. In the 1990s, Geoff co-created the Topgrading® brand of talent management.

As a social entrepreneur, Geoff is the Founding Chairman of two 501(c)(3) not-for-profit organizations. SMARTKids Leadership Program provides a customized program of ten years of leadership tutoring and a $100,000 scholarship to top students with leadership potential from low-income communities. Secondly, The Leaders Initiative seeks to elevate humanity by identifying, developing, and deploying society's greatest leaders into government. Geoff and his ghSMART colleagues volunteer as leadership advisors in the fields of education, public health, and government.

Geoff earned a B.A. in economics with honors from Northwestern University, an M.A., and a Ph.D. in psychology from Claremont Graduate University, where he was mentored by Peter F. Drucker. Geoff was elected to Sigma Xi, the honorary society for holders of doctoral degrees, and is a member of the Young Presidents' Organization.

RANDY STREET

Randy Street is the Managing Partner of ghSMART.

Randy has served as a leadership advisor to boards, CEOs, and executive teams for more than two decades. He is an internationally acclaimed keynote speaker with a dynamic and energetic style that motivates people to perform at their very best.

In collaboration with Geoff Smart, the firm's CEO, Randy co-authored *Who: The A Method for Hiring* (Random House, 2008), which is a *New York Times, Wall Street Journal, Business-Week, USA Today,* and *Publishers Weekly* bestseller. He has been featured in *The Wall Street Journal, BusinessWeek,* and other leading publications.

Upon release, *Who* became the number-one bestseller on Amazon.com out of 24 million titles, and hit every major bestseller list in the United States. Soundview Executive Book Summaries gave *Who* the "Best 30 Business Books Award," *Shanghai Daily* named it a "Top 5 Best Business Book in China," and Canada's *Globe and Mail* named *Who* the "#1 Best Business and Management Book of 2009."

Prior to joining ghSMART, Randy was the Executive Vice President of Sales and Marketing and Executive Vice President of Corporate Development and Strategy for EzGov, a software firm that was named the fastest-growing company in Atlanta during his tenure. Before that, Randy was a strategy consultant with Bain & Company, where he led projects and advised senior executives of Global 1000 companies in a wide range of industries.

Randy earned his MBA from Harvard Business School and a B.S. in mechanical engineering from Rice University.

ALAN FOSTER

Alan is a Consultant at ghSMART. He serves private equity investors, Fortune 500 clients, and nonprofit organizations in the areas of leadership selection, development, and organizational transformation.

Prior to joining ghSMART, Alan was a senior manager with Bain & Company in their New York and London offices. Over his twelve years at Bain, Alan worked in more than twenty industries, which included financial services, consumer products, technology, and private equity. He led teams that assisted clients in turning around operational performance, building high-performance cultures, and evaluating major acquisitions. Alan also led projects to reinforce Bain's global culture of coaching and apprenticeship across forty-two offices and redesigned their approach to employee engagement. He also enjoys working with a number of leading nonprofit organizations on strategic talent issues.

Alan graduated with honors in economics from Cambridge University, and earned his MBA from INSEAD in France and his master's in applied positive psychology from the University of Pennsylvania.

About the Type

This book was set in Minion, a 1990 Adobe Originals typeface by Robert Slimbach. Minion is inspired by classical, old-style typefaces of the late Renaissance, a period of elegant and beautiful type designs. Created primarily for text setting, Minion combines the aesthetic and functional qualities that make text type highly readable with the versatility of digital technology.

Wallet Card